RECOVERING LIFE

Searching for
a Healthy Spirituality
for the Whole of our Humanity

COLIN HOLMES

PESIOD
Eager & Earnest

Editor: Paul B Coulter

Copyeditor: Christine Memory

Cover design: Paul Davies

First published 2023

ISBN: 9798398071542

I dedicate this book to my wife, Ally.

By my side in the shadows long enough,
Might now be your time to shine.

CONTENTS

Introduction 1

1. Recovering in Nature 9
2. Recovering with Friends 23
3. Recovering my Body 37
4. Recovering our Hearts 49
5. Recovering our Balance 63
6. Recovering in Seasons of Life 76
7. Recovering in the Dark 89

Conclusion 101

Acknowledgments 108

Endnotes 112

INTRODUCTION

How did it come to this?

Lightning strikes
(Saturday 11th July 2020. Co. Armagh, N. Ireland.)

How did it come to this? Here I was on the middle Saturday of a family holiday. The journeys for the day were for adventure on mountain bike trails with my eldest son. I looked forward to downhill dirt tracks and the satisfaction of coming back covered in mud, content and closer in our shared enjoyment. It was a day that promised the feeling of freewheeling freedom.

Instead, the bumps and jumps, the twists and turns, were made in the back of an ambulance as I was rushed to the local hospital. Then, instead of freewheeling freedom, I was wheeled into the confines of a CT scanner, which revealed I'd suffered a bleed on my brain. No family by my side today, due to cruel Covid restrictions. They were brought to mind by a nurse seeking to bring me encouragement. Sadly, this didn't have the desired effect. Rather it troubled me, as the fear flashed across my mind of never seeing them again. Lightning had struck.

I had suffered a 2.3cm haemorrhage around my cerebellum, an area of the brain responsible for balance and coordination. So, the next ambulance journey to the neurosurgical ward in Belfast was far from easy. The driver was smooth, but it felt like the roughest ride of my life.

Our holidays had been a joyous series of reunions with family and friends. We were enjoying a world opening up after being locked down. How glorious to get together after being apart for too long. In this expanding world my own world suddenly became very small. I was most comfortable with my eyes closed, body stilled, in silence. The festival of life had been interrupted by the shadow of death.

I was used to being healthy in my forty years to this point. This was the closest I had been to death's door. Although I felt mostly calm, I knew this period was critical. There was always the possibility of a rebleed. I could take nothing for granted.

The timing wasn't lost on me either. This was the day in Northern Ireland when some people light bonfires before parading on 12th July. I grew up in the midst of these fires, but they failed to ignite anything in me. What was a mild and rainy day outside was the day in which I encountered a lightning strike. I had been knocked off my feet and a fire had been lit in my head. Little did I know it would rekindle a deeper recovery that warmed my heart and soul.

It was also twenty two years since I'd started going out with my wife, Ally. The thought of not seeing her again scared me. I'm glad to say what lay ahead would rekindle my love for her. My eyes would be opened to who really mattered in my life. My wife - always by my side, yet too easily taken for granted. My three kids - too often ignored in the distractedness of an overbusy life. Our precious family who shared life around the dinner table - where I could be physically present but all too often absent minded.

Covid clouds roll in
(Friday 12th March 2020. Waterford, Ireland.)

How did it come to this? Four months earlier, I was in Waterford when the children of Ireland were told to stay at home. It had just gotten very real.

It had been coming. Stories from Wuhan moved closer to Northern Italy, then into Dublin. Now it was making its presence felt in our own homes. The children were to be off school for a period of at least two weeks... which turned into almost five months!

The next week, March 17th, would normally see us join the crowds on the streets of Waterford for St. Patrick's Day. This time they were empty, as we all stayed at home in an effort to protect each other. The clouds of Covid had rolled in and we prepared ourselves for an emergency which might last months rather than weeks. Little would we know there would be a further St Patrick's Day, in 2021, where everyone stayed at home. Our recovery would be longer than initially expected. Not even months, but years.

Coming into 2020 it seemed impossible that anything could displace Brexit from the news cycle. Now, rather than discussions around geographical borders, especially on the island of Ireland, the focus was on trying to draw a border around this virus. By March 27th the first lockdown was in place.

We had hoped we might carry on with life and contain this virus. Now it was containing us. Our world had become small. We were socially distanced and kept apart from others physically like never before. As the number of cases and hospitalisations grew, so did the mortalities. On a daily basis we were informed of these numbers, bringing the shadow of death closer to our door than we are normally used to.

So, as the first wave of Covid rose, I found myself overwhelmed. I tried to stay on top of the rising seas of information on social media and news feeds. I was treading water, as the waves of anxiety were rising around me. We were going under, fighting for breath. Whilst this virus was new on the scene, rising levels of anxiety and time spent on technology were not.

The winds of change are blowing
(Saturday 27 April 2019. Ireland.)

How did it come to this? A hectic pace of living, skimming along the surface, whilst being anxious and unsettled underneath are far from what the contented and comfortable benefits of consumerism offer us. Yet sadly they were features I recognised all too readily from those I journeyed through life with. They were the scenes I surveyed, as I saw the lives surrounding me.

Fascination gripped me, as I opened the Saturday newspaper to be greeted with another survey which put words and figures on this. An enjoyable part of my day off is being drawn into the many portions of the newspaper, as it offers fresh perspectives on life and culture. On this day I was far from disappointed. My reading pace quickened as I devoured the findings of, 'The Signs of the Times Survey', which put numbers and figures on the cultural change that Ireland had seen over the previous ten years.[1] I was excited, not because I'm a numbers geek, but rather because what I sensed in the culture I lived in was shown in these statistics. It rang true. What I saw around me matched what I was reading in front of me.

It was a year before Covid clouds rolled in, but there were already signs of lives being overwhelmed by digital connections. We were scrolling on the surface, but it was leaving a mark underneath. There were also signs of cracks in our seemingly comfortable consumerist society.

Reflecting on the findings, Fintan O Toole suggested life for many was like a swimming duck, which looked like it was gliding smoothly on the water, but beneath the surface was working very hard to do so. It seems even those who are happy with their comfortable lifestyles are far from happy about what it is costing them to achieve this.

As a country we had sought freedom from religion; expressed particularly in referenda on same sex marriage and abortion. Ireland was moving on from its religious past. This transformation had caused cracks underneath the new found confidence in a more socially liberal society, as many people were unsettled by the changes.

In all of this Ireland is moving, in its own particular way, to being increasingly secular and post-Christian. A shift that is occurring across the Western world. Could these rapid changes in culture be connected to the fast moving pace of our lives? We are increasingly hurried, hustled and hectic. Could it be that the winds of cultural change have blown anxiety and stress across our lives? It was never meant to be like this.

Whatever the weather
(Today, wherever you are.)

Let me extend to you the invitation that came to me in my hospital bed. In a strange, surprising, and sudden way in the hospital I had a sense I was being invited graciously to rest. I was being sat down to reflect, recover, and be refreshed. I had been knocked back off my feet for now.

Words came to me that would provide the permission to rest, and the pattern and pathway that I should take in doing this.

> In repentance and rest is your salvation,
> in quietness and trust is your strength,
> Isaiah 30:15.

The verse, from the Old Testament in the Bible, made sense of my present physical limitations. In my dizziness and lack of balance it was in being sat down to rest and in quietness that I felt strongest. Yet, it also called me to reflect upon a busyness of life and self-dependence that was to be set aside. This was the road to return to who was important and to trust in help that came from beyond myself. It would be in this that I would know recovery that was more than physical, but also relational, emotional, and even spiritual.

As I extend the invitation to you to read this book, I

want to be honest from the start. My journey of rest and recovery helped me recover life as I trusted God was in this. This book is written from a Christian perspective. It is not, however, a book intended only for those who are convinced of this perspective. It is not insisting you must believe, but rather inviting you to consider Jesus afresh.

As you read its pages, I'd invite you to take time to step aside from your hurry, hustle, and hectic pace. Let's sit down and slowly reflect on life.

So, I invite you to join me on the journey, as I will share my own particular health journey of rest and recovery. I will also share observations of the common Covid clouds we all journeyed under, as well as the winds of anxiety and stress that blow across our lives, in our changing culture not only in Ireland, but across the Western world.

Haven't we been talking about Covid long enough though? Surely we can put it behind us and move on with life? Let me suggest that the best way to do this lies, not in denying it ever came our way, but rather by reflecting and recognising some of the strange gifts it presented us with. Then we might be free to travel further down the road, without being unknowingly weighed down with its baggage.

We will begin our journey in the opening three chapters by recognising some of the cracks that came to the surface as I was recovering my health. I found myself disconnected from nature, from friends, and even from my own body. So I came to appreciate afresh the most vital human connections. In chapters four to seven I will share help for the recovery road in the wonderful wisdom books of the Bible - Psalms, Proverbs, Ecclesiastes and Job. These were valued friends and trusted guides to me as I journeyed through difficult times. Each of these wisdom books will be paired with one of the Gospels, as we journey with Jesus into recovering life.

To help you reflect and weave this book into your own story there is at the end of each chapter a poem, some questions to move you to practice, and a prayer.

These are written in extension of the reality that we are not just beings busy with thoughts and feelings on the inside, but with full hands on the outside and who all together are living souls, woven together in our complex and beautifully fragile humanity.

In light of this, the reflections at the close of the chapters seek to move us from just reading to thinking, feeling, doing, trusting, and connecting to a story bigger than our own small selves.

In the telling of stories and the penning of poems my hope is that these words capture something of the place they are written from, the island of Ireland; rich in the tradition of those who have a way with words. My own origin story is found in Co. Antrim in Northern Ireland / the North. This recovery story begins there too, but for the majority is found in Co. Waterford in the Republic of Ireland / Ireland. For those familiar with the contested and complicated history of this place you will have picked up the complexities in even naming where I'm from! Whether you're from this island or further afield, I make no apologies for writing with a flavour of this place. My hope is that overall it might be a help and not a hindrance as you journey with me.

It is my hope this book might help you find your own way to being refreshed in life. My personal journey involved a five month period of recovering my health. As you are invited to slow down and reflect you might be struggling to find five minutes, never mind five months! Such a lengthy time period is far from essential for our travels together, nor would I wish it on you to be honest. The chapters that follow will describe pathways to recovering life travelled by many more than me. People from a wide range of circumstances. If you are currently rushed off your feet or you've been set back off them, come as you are and reflect in whatever way best works for you.

Let's begin this journey together in our shared humanity, beautiful yet broken and in need of recovering life. We set out in a common search for a healthy spirituality for the whole of our humanity.

Poem - Sanctuary of Sink

Sanctuary of sink
follows raucous table roar
gives space and time to think
to chew the cud, for mind to soar
while feet are at a standstill
hands and heart by water warmed
made strong in company or lone, until
the dishes done, the shelter's gone -
Let's brave the storm!

Question

Where might you find sanctuary - a safe time and place - to slow down and reflect as you read this book?

Prayer

Lord, we bring you the unexpected and unexplained interruptions in our lives.
We leave before you the "How did it come to this?" moments,
and ask for ears to hear your gracious invitation to rest.
In our returning and resting, our quieting and trusting,
Gracious God might you save and strengthen,
heal and help,
restore and refresh.
That we might live more freely and lightly we pray.

CHAPTER 1

RECOVERING IN NATURE

Garden Rest in the Wastelands

**You will be like a well-watered garden,
like a spring whose waters never fail.
Isaiah 58:11b**

In search of the garden

My appreciation of our garden in Spring 2020 was in full bloom. When the lockdown came our way we were greeted with a sustained spell of dry weather; soon after we discovered new walks and woods hidden within our 2km limits. It was just what we needed, to get out and breathe the fresh air as the world closed in.

As the traffic stopped and the world fell silent, I heard the bird song like never before. Had the birds come closer since human hurry and hustle ceased? Or had they always been singing and falling on deaf ears, my mind noisy with its own preoccupations? Being more conscious and connected to the beauty of nature in our neighbourhood proved a welcome refuge as Covid waves surged.

Your experience may well have been different. Restrictions and opportunities for garden rest differed. Some were starved of such outdoor freshness, being closed up inside. Friends we have in Spain seemed to be

9

particularly restricted. If it's true we only really appreciate something when it's gone, maybe a newfound appreciation for the garden was also growing in these confining circumstances. Hopefully you can think of moments when this estrangement ended and you were reacquainted with the outdoors.

We always seem to fare better as a family outdoors. It is the place we are most ourselves and most together. For our three kids it allows space to exercise, it provides a playground to enjoy, and a wonderland of plants and animals to explore. When indoors, tensions and pressures build. It's outdoors we find welcome release. So we often find ourselves in search of the garden of the great outdoors. It's written into the story of our family.

My own love of the outdoors finds its origins even further back. Both my grandas worked the land. My mum's dad was a farmer. My dad's dad worked in the forestry service. Although I have no memories of being at their side in farm or forest, somehow their story has left its mark. I've discovered, like so many on this island of Ireland, that I'm much closer to the land than I might realise. My roots lie in the garden.

This movement back towards the land lies beyond my own family story and was well underway before Covid called. The search for the garden is a path well travelled.

The Grow it Yourself movement encourages people towards their garden to grow their own food. The aim is to support people to live happier, healthier, and more sustainable lives by developing a deeper connection with their food. The journey began when Michael, who was an IT salesman, popped into the shop to buy some garlic. As he read the label, 'Product of China' it gave him reason to pause...before leaving the shop with the seeds of an idea from which GIY grew. The garlic had been on an epic five thousand mile journey and Michael was moved to embark on a journey of his own.

Many others have been journeying through the great garden of the outdoors on two wheels, cycling the greenways which wind across the country. The Waterford Greenway offers 46km of relaxing cycling on the flat that has proven attractive to people of a wide range of ages and fitnesses. The journey begins in Waterford City beside the River Suir and then moves through green fields with the Comeragh mountains in the background. At the finish it brings you beside the sea and sand to its close in Dungarvan. The joy of healthy exercise, at a slow pace, in the fresh air, with beautiful scenery. It's a journey worth making.

The growing community who have taken the plunge into sea swimming, have also found their way back to nature. The TV documentary, shown on RTE, 'Vitamin Sea' follows the story of eight people who have found a deep connection with the water.[2] They are reinvigorated and revived - finding health for body and mind. It is a place of refreshment, but also of refuge for some who are recovering from loss and trauma in their lives. Freedom and safety are found in the waters of the garden.

In our search for the garden we've been putting down roots and drawing freshness from the world around us.

The origins of garden rest

What is it about the garden, or a day spent in a park, that brings us peace and happiness? What is it that draws us into the outdoors when we need to rest and relax? Why is a walk outside so good for us? Could it be an echo that sounds from our very origins, written into the family story of humanity?

The origin story the Bible presents fits with our longing for the garden. So, I'd like to invite you to come with me and take a walk in Eden garden. For some, I recognise your pathway may be difficult underfoot. You'll need to step over divisive debates about the origins of life. You'll need to find a way around a belief that the Bible's ideas of beginnings are fanciful and unscientific. To help you find your way, we'll not be focusing on timings or the exact process. Rather, we'll leave aside the *when* and the details of *how*, to look at the *who* and the *where*. Indeed, this fits with the nature of the story we find in the book of Genesis, in which the author is more concerned with *who* created than our more modern question of *how*.

We'll go together then to the first page of the first book, Genesis, the book of beginnings, to the garden where it all began.

> Now the Lord God had planted a garden in the east, in Eden; and there he put the man he had formed. The Lord God made all kinds of trees grow out of the ground—trees that were pleasing to the eye and good for food. In the middle of the garden were the tree of life and the tree of the knowledge of good and evil. A river watering the garden flowed from Eden…
> Genesis 2:8-10.

This garden was a place of beauty and goodness. Trees planted, with fruit that pleased the eye, satisfied the stomach and would sustain life. In the previous chapter of Genesis, the parallel account of the creation finishes each day with the refrain, "And God saw it was good." This is surpassed on the final day with the joyous, "God saw all that he had made and it was very good." This is captured in the name of the garden, 'Eden', meaning delight and pleasure. Here we have a very good beginning.

The man is placed in a garden, which had been planted and planned in an orderly way by the hands of a Master Gardener. So, we are connected to the garden, but also to the Gardener and, before too long, to one another. Our origins in the garden describe our deepest connections as humans. Here is where we might truly thrive.

This was a garden that was full of life and life filling. As humans we were planted in the garden so that we might thrive and be fruitful, as we take care of it. The garden was the place of work, rest, and play. The place we are to call home.

Far from garden rest

Today however, our lives are far from flourishing. Whilst I've never experienced an abrupt episode of burnout, I've been too close for comfort on too many occasions. For ten years, from 2010 to 2020, I worked part-time as a pharmacist in the community and also part-time in a Christian church in pastoral, youth, and community work. Both the charity and healthcare sectors are well known for being places of high stress and where workers might experience burnout.

I loved the work and the people, but there were periods when the demands and busyness meant I felt somewhat drained or detached from the people I was serving. I was disconnected. I was close to burnout.

I was also close to burnout because, in both the pharmacy and church, I was working alongside and supporting those who displayed various shapes and signs of burnout. They were overwhelmed or exhausted emotionally, physically, and mentally. Too many of those beside me had to take prolonged breaks from work or change to different jobs. There were also those who showed remarkable endurance to keep going, but with a significant effort in struggling to survive. I so wished that for them it could have been different. Whilst my support was well intended and often well received, there were also times when I likely made things worse rather than better. I brought my own share of mess as we shared life together. It was a struggle.

Whilst nature around us may be alive, we ourselves are barely surviving, never mind thriving. We may feel exhausted, the very life drained from us. How can it be on an island with so many shades of verdant green, we seem to be withering away, disconnected from nature?

Could it be that the factory has got in the way? Has consumerism led us to prize profit and productivity above all else? This in turn leaves us drained from life and far from flourishing. An observer from farther West in the USA, Jefferson Bethke, has suggested that the beginning of our hustle culture was when the assembly line was born.[3] Even if we haven't worked a day in our lives in the factory, it seems the factory has worked its way into our rhythms and way of life.

The results are far from pretty. Walking a path determined by the fastest and easiest way to what we really want, leads us into barren wastelands. Litter lies across our path as the craving for food has been met and the waste discarded. Ugly and uniform buildings are thrown up in car parks on the edge of town, fast and functional, the quickest route to sell us what we really want. Zombies roam the streets, as we are exhausted from overspending our energy and time for what we seemingly want. Life is drained of colour and joy, it is grim and grey. We have made a home in the wilderness. The wilderness has made its home in us.

> …like a bush in the wastelands;
> they will not see when prosperity comes.
> They will dwell in the parched places of the desert,
> in a salt land where no one lives.
> Jeremiah 17:6.

This is the poetic picture the prophet Jeremiah uses to describe those who, "…trust in man, who draws strength from mere flesh and whose heart turns away from the Lord." (Jeremiah 17:5.) There are those who were disconnected from the well of living waters. The wilderness in them was because they had turned away from the Lord as their source of life.

As a prophet, Jeremiah's role was to speak God's word to call his people, Israel, back to himself. His book is a collection of his writings during the seventh and sixth centuries before Christ. This covers the period in which God's people were exiled from their homeland. It was a troubled time with the people of Israel dislocated and distanced from their homeland. There was a turbulent time of transition that was testing. This only brought the true nature of their 'heartland' to light.

> The heart is deceitful above all things
>   and beyond cure.
>   Who can understand it?
> "I the Lord search the heart
> and examine the mind,
> to reward each person according to their conduct,
>   according to what their deeds deserve."
> Jeremiah 17:9-10.

Today we also live in turbulent times. What has the turmoil of changes in our culture, with the resulting dislocations and distance, revealed about the crop growing in our own hearts and lives? Do we find ourselves faced with the uncomfortable truth that we're barely surviving or maybe even dying inside?

Thriving in the garden

There is another way, though. A way of living that results in growth even when we face the heat, that is vibrant when we encounter stress in life.

> ...a tree planted by the water
> that sends out its roots by the stream.
> It does not fear when heat comes;
> its leaves are always green.
> It has no worries in a year of drought
> and never fails to bear fruit.

This picture of life which Jeremiah describes, comes from being connected to God: '...the one who trusts in the Lord, whose confidence is in him.' (Jeremiah 17:7-8).

Such language of life under the heat of the sun is also found on the lips of Jesus.

I am the vine; you are the branches. If you remain in me and I in you, you will bear much fruit; apart from me you can do nothing… If you keep my commands, you will remain in my love, just as I have kept my Father's commands and remain in his love. I have told you this so that my joy may be in you and that your joy may be complete.   My command is this: love each other as I have loved you.   Greater love has no one than this: to lay down one's life for one's friends.
John 15:5, 10-13.

Thriving for both Jeremiah and Jesus is found in a life that bears fruit.   Both voices echo the beauty and goodness of the garden in the beginning.

This goodness was brought home to me on a walk with our children in Mount Congreve, a beautiful garden outside our home town of Waterford.   One of our children, a big fan of apples, was captivated.   As he saw the apples on the trees his eyes were wide with wonder. Imagine his delight when one of the gardeners offered him a huge one to eat. It was nearly as big as his head, but that didn't put him off. Even now he often eats two apples a day. If one is meant to keep the doctor away, I always wonder what might two achieve? For him the apples are not only good to look at, but to be tasted and eaten.

Isn't it the same with the fruitful life Jesus describes? A life connected to him flows out in loving connections to others also. Such love is described by Jesus as laying down your life for your friends.   Not long after speaking these words, Jesus displayed such love, as he died for those he loved on the cross.   The fruit of such selfless and sacrificial love is attractive.   This involves a costly self-denial, which is described in Christian terms as dying to ourselves, but for all this it is life-giving to others. When we see these qualities in others they are not only attractive to the eye, but pleasing to the palate and nourishing to our souls.

An even broader description, we might even call it a

breakfast buffet, of this fruit is provided by Paul as he writes to a church in Galatia, which is in modern day Turkey, encouraging them to live freely as Christians. 'But the fruit of the Spirit is love, joy, peace, forbearance, kindness, goodness, faithfulness, gentleness and self-control.' (Galatians 5:23).

Each of these qualities is displayed best of all in Jesus. Might this Jesus-like fruit also be close to what we aspire to be and to offer to others?

Such is the attractive contrast that Jesus' people offer today. In a world unsettled by the speed of change in the moral fabric of culture, Jesus' people hold firm to their convictions, even when they are unpopular. They are faithful. Where there are those who are isolated and lonely, Jesus' people show compassion and kindness. They are loving. When immigrants or asylum seekers are treated unfairly, Jesus' people speak up for justice. They are true. Such fruit is pleasing to the eye and good enough to feast on.

It seems not only do we find life in the garden, but garden life has found its way into us. The goodness of the garden grows, as the fruit of love blossoms. How different this is from the factory that operates in us, prizing profits and productivity. What a contrast from the life that is withering away in the wilderness, disconnected from God.

Here also, is a very different perspective on Jesus. Far from inhibiting our freedom and enjoyment of life, to be connected to Jesus is joyful and life giving. It is to flourish and bear the fruit of love. Could it be that we are withering in the wilderness because we have left Jesus behind us? We are branches that are disconnected from him and, just as Jesus says, we wither and die because we do not remain in him.

Jesus is the Vine. When we have made our home in his love and life, this is where we truly thrive. We bear the fruit of love and life. These are never more gratefully received than when we are on the road to recovery.

Recovering in the garden

My appreciation of the great garden of the outdoors blossomed even more from Summer 2020, as I began a period of rest and recovery following the sudden and unexpected bleed on my brain. I had been knocked back off my feet and would spend most of the remainder of the year recovering my strength. Although I live in Waterford, in Ireland's South East, my brain bleed had occurred during holidays in Northern Ireland / the North. So the journey of recovery began in the company of family in the fresh air of the majestic Mourne Mountains in Co. Down.

I had grown up with the solitary and sacred mountain of Slemish in Co. Antrim as a view from our house. This is the place where, tradition suggests, a young Patrick minded sheep in the cold, whilst his heart was warmed in prayer to God. When I married a woman from Co. Down she threw cold water on my Slemish love: sure it was only a hill! Nothing could surpass her beloved Mournes. She wasn't alone in her love. The creator of Narnia, C.S. Lewis, is said to have taken inspiration for his magical land from the Mountains of Mourne. As I recovered in their company, my own appreciation of them deepened.

The Mournes formed the moving picture as I sat in the garden to rest. They were the panorama as I slowly increased my length of walks and improved my balance. A river nearby was my first trip out with family as my circle slowly increased. My senses were alive as I walked outdoors. Was it the freshness that follows a major health event or just the slowness of my pace enabling my senses to soak in their surroundings? I was more conscious and more connected to nature. I was travelling lighter and enjoying garden rest.

Immersing ourselves in the garden of the outdoors can be good for body, mind, and soul. The Japanese art of forest bathing is all about soaking in the atmosphere of the forest by mindful walking. Since the term emerged in Japan in the 1980's it has spread across the globe. We can find health and healing outdoors.

Such healing balm is part of the picture of the great garden at the conclusion of the human story in the Scriptures. Just as the very good beginning of the human story was placed in the garden, so is the even better ending. In Revelation 22:1-2 we read:

> Then the angel showed me the river of the water of life, as clear as crystal, flowing from the throne of God and of the Lamb down the middle of the great street of the city. On each side of the river stood the tree of life, bearing twelve crops of fruit, yielding its fruit every month. And the leaves of the tree are for the healing of the nations.

This is the continued description of what John, the disciple of Jesus who wrote Revelation, calls the new heaven and the new earth. It is Eden-like with rivers of water, and living and fruitful trees, all in the company of the master Gardener and Creator, God himself, who sits on the throne.

The leaves for healing of the nations are an echo of words spoken by the prophet Ezekiel to illustrate the temple of the Lord being rebuilt after being devastated in the time of exile. The temple was the house of the Lord, where God was at home. It recalls the garden imagery of Eden. So here, God himself is at home again with his people. What greater healing could there be?

This is the place of fullness of life in the end. God makes his home with us in a new heaven and new earth. This is far from the detached, disembodied ideas of a life beyond death as spirits in the clouds in heaven. It is here we find a heavenly hope that is much more earthy and grounded. In the end we can enjoy life in the garden for which we were made.

Such joy is only found because the garden itself has been recovered. We live in a world that knows disease and decay, disaster and death. So we endure bleeds on the brain and global pandemics. We live for now in the shadow of death. The Bible describes this as being under the curse that has fallen on the world due to a turning away from God in the garden in the very opening chapters of the story. In the end however, the Lamb is seated on the throne. The Lamb who has taken away the sin of the world, Jesus. He is the one who has taken the curse and tasted death to bring healing. His presence on the throne shows he has been wounded, yet has emerged victorious. In the end there is a recovery and renewal. As John says 'He will wipe every tear from their eyes. There will be no more death or mourning or crying or pain, for the old order of things has passed away.' (Revelation 21:4).

So, the garden lies at the very good origin and the even better ending of our story as human beings. As we find ourselves in the middle of the story of our lives, it is no surprise that we find life in the great garden of the outdoors.

If then we are to set off in search of recovering life, the garden of the outdoors is a great place to start. There are many ways for us to do this practically. If much of your time is spent in front of a screen and connecting digitally with people you might make time to get outside for a walk on your break to change the scenery. If you live in an urban environment you might escape to the country on your days off, or to the park on your lunch break, or even bring the garden indoors into your living space with flowers and plants. If you have periods of intense busyness you might make an effort to balance this with some freshness in the outdoors planned into your diary. It could be as simple as choosing to walk some of the way home and doing this slower than usual to savour your surroundings.

As we make our way along the paths of everyday life, the simple graces of the garden of nature are God's invitation to us to rest and enjoy the life that comes from being rooted in Jesus. To leave behind the wasteland of our hustle and rest in the garden.

Poem - Autumn Twilight

Littered leaves underfoot,
Poet's easy pickings.
Crunch to ear, food for roots,
This season makes the soul sing.

Summer's verdant green,
Forty shades in one
Take their leave, changing scene
As glowing colours run.

I'm singing in the leaves,
'Falling Slowly' down,
'Moment-stuck' I hardly breath,
The carpet soaks the ground.

Heart hard, open cracked,
Like tree-fall conker bounty.
Inside - surprise eyes have lacked
In humdrum round and rounding.

Summer's glory gone,
Nights draw quick to close,
The day reflected on,
The year's twilight repose.

Questions

1. Where have you found the joy of being connected to the great garden of the outdoors?
2. How is the garden of your life currently; dying, surviving or thriving? What signs of the wilderness or of the garden have made their home in you?
3. How does Jesus' picture of thriving - as the Vine and branches - compare with your perception of Christianity?
4. What might be the next steps in growing in Jesus-like fruitfulness?
5. How might you practise time spent enjoying the simple graces of the garden and the rest it offers?

Prayer

In our worried world, full of disease, disaster and death,
help us, Jesus, to walk with you in the garden.
Open our eyes, minds and hearts to consider
the birds, who do not sow or reap or store in barns, yet are fed by their Father,
and the flowers, clothed in beauty by their good God,
that we might know the Father's care for us, as part of his creation,
and enjoy gracious garden rest
and grow Jesus-like fruit in us that others would find attractive, tasty and life-giving.

CHAPTER TWO

RECOVERING WITH FRIENDS

Soul Friends over Facebook friends.

...but there is a friend who sticks closer than a brother.
Proverbs 18:24b

Feeling the distance

The joy of reconnecting was upon us. The summer of 2020 saw precious reunions between friends and family, as Ireland emerged out the other side of the first wave of Covid. Too long I'd been talking through screens on digital devices to those I dearly loved. Too long I'd been missing the easy company of being with good friends. Too long I'd been kept at a distance from those in hospital in need of encouragement. Whilst some of these connections were recovered, others remained incomplete, but one thing was certain, I'd been distanced too long.

Any wonder then, that I said an unfond farewell to the loss of company and the isolation of Covid's prolonged restrictions and harsh lockdowns. None of us do too well on our own for too long.

Distanced by disease

It was in this summer of reconnecting that I was to suffer a further distancing from those I loved most. The unexpected bleed on my brain saw me removed from family in an ambulance and in hospital with limited visits for almost a week. The joy of reconnecting with my kids when discharged was special. It also proved difficult. I had limited energy and tolerance for noise, strong feelings, and conversation, all areas in which our children excel! At the beginning I spent most of the day on my own. I would choose when I could spend time with my family based on my capacity. I was feeling the distance.

On returning home to Waterford, in August, I had also travelled further down the road of recovery. Now, I was feeling the distance in a different way. At the beginning of September, information from Headway Ireland, who give support and provide services for people with acquired brain injury, brought fresh light on my recovery. The hidden aspects of brain injury such as my concentration, communication, and ability to handle my own emotions and those of others, were brought into the open. Sadly, this was proving most difficult for the woman at my side, Ally. As well as being tired out from taking on more with our three kids and having the weight of worry about my own recovery, she was living with a husband who didn't seem to be himself. Communication and emotions were too often strained. It would take a while for her to recognise me as being, 'back to my old self again'. In the meantime we were both feeling the distance.

In the same period, I also carried a feeling of unease and discomfort that was more of a slow burner. The pain of being distanced from family had been acute. The missing of church friends was more gradual and chronic. Even when restrictions fell away to allow for happy reunions, my health limitations remained in the way. Again I was feeling the distance.

Distance disrupted

We are no strangers to feeling the distance. It is not merely confined to periods of ill health or to a global pandemic. Social distancing was a familiar and well founded reality in our lives long before the phrase emerged with Covid. We are divided from our closest neighbours, living separate lives fenced in our own gardens, closed behind our own doors, locked to our own screens. Such distance was disrupted when Covid came to call. Had our hurry from the front door to the car commute been interrupted long enough to permit human interaction and conversation? Maybe we even learned one another's names!

At a time of distance from friends and extended family, I discovered a newfound closeness and moving towards neighbours. As many were at home more and exercising close to their house, there was a chance to connect more with those beside us. Everyone in our own house found real encouragement in a tough time in being with families around us and knowing the freshness of getting to know people more. Our neighbourly distance had been disrupted.

There was also much more time together as a family under the one roof. For us there was homeschooling as well as working from home. There was less going our separate ways and running from one activity to the next through the week. We could share in each other's days more. The kids got to see what our work involved and we got to be closer to them as they were learning new things from school. The distance within our own family had been disrupted.

Overall we'd been socially rearranged. Brought closer to some, as well as more distant from others.

Digitally distanced

This rearrangement was never truer than in our newfound world of digital connections. As a church we decided to meet together on Zoom from the beginning, which allowed us to see and hear one another, to be in conversation and support one another. We moved closer to one another. In the early days of Zoom this connection was gratefully received. As time went on however, it led to more of a mixed response.

There were some who seemed to come alive on Zoom, they moved towards the screen. Then there were those who moved away from the screen, or would turn the screen off, or would fall away from Zoom in time. What provided a great way of staying in touch was at the same time an irritatingly unsatisfying way of connecting with one another.

Zoom certainly provided us with humour at a time when laughs were hard to come by. There were the unexpected cameos in work meetings from other house residents, be they children or pets. There were the awkward moments of someone talking freely not realising they were unmuted. Then of course there was the time when people discovered the backgrounds with all the fun they could bring to the party.

For all this humour, there were the times of poor connection, frozen screens and missing words. The talking over one another and not being able to listen well. The inability to read body language and to be with one another. The annoyingly easy option of being continually fascinated with your own familiar face rather than taking in another's!

Could it be that connecting with each other on Zoom provided the best and also some of the worst times of our time in lockdown? This hybrid experience of moving closer to others, whilst feeling farther apart is also evident on social media. The readily accessible connections with so many friends at the touch of the button on devices carried on our person at all times, was more valuable than ever during a time of social distancing. This all comes with the gratification of not only knowing you're valued, but being able to put a number on it, as we count views and likes, friends and followers. Seemingly instant affirmation... which so quickly can turn to obsessively insecure posturing. Are these my real friends? Can I really share the real me?

Could it be that our digital connections are leaving us more disconnected? In our attempts for closeness are we distanced from one another even more?

Distanced in the land of welcomes

Our communities had been feeling the distance before Covid arrived. The loneliness epidemic predates the coronavirus pandemic.

I've been living in Ireland's sunny South-East for over thirteen years now. I've been living at a distance from family and from close friends who I grew up with. Sharing my formative years and memories from school and college, they understand me and are familiar with the real me. Whilst I've known the welcome and warmth of a community of people who are friendly, at times I have felt isolated, as it seems not so many really want to make friends. I've also worked alongside families who've moved to this country and lived here for significant stretches of time, yet have really struggled to make many close friends. Deep friendships are hard to find.

In his book, 'The Irish Paradox', Sean Moncrieff describes friendship among Irish people as full of contradictions.[4] As a returning emigrant, he writes this from a place of painful experience and describes how the Irish are both outgoing and friendly, and yet can also be closed. He also suggests the welcome afforded to people also depends on how well they are known and connected to an area. In the land of a hundred thousand welcomes, with a sense of genuinely warm friendliness, how can it still be so difficult to make good friends?

Finding a Soul Friend

In another age in Ireland such deep friendships were named and cherished. In ancient Celtic tradition a soul friend was known as your *anam cara*. Someone who you could trust with your deepest secrets and who would stick by you over a lifetime. You shared a deep connection. As Christianity developed in Ireland, the choosing of a priest to whom you would confess your sins was less determined by professional qualifications and more by being an *anam cara*. They would hear the depths of your darkest sin and shame yet not judge or walk away.

Such closeness and the beauty of such deep friendship are described in the biblical wisdom book of Proverbs.

A friend loves at all times,
and a brother is born for a time of adversity.
Proverbs 17:17.

One who has unreliable friends soon comes to ruin,
but there is a friend who sticks closer than a brother.
Proverbs 18:24.

Wounds from a friend can be trusted,
but an enemy multiplies kisses.
Proverbs 27:6.

Perfume and incense bring joy to the heart,
and the pleasantness of a friend
springs from their heartfelt advice.
Proverbs 27:9.

A friend whose love is constant, stays close, gives heartfelt advice, and is unafraid to speak hard words for our own good is to be prized. They can be trusted.

During his time on earth, Jesus spent much of his time pouring into the lives of a small group he called friends. His greatest act of love would be to lay down his life for his friends, an example they were to imitate.

My command is this: Love each other as I have loved you. Greater love has no one than this: to lay down one's life for one's friends. You are my friends if you do what I command. I no longer call you servants, because a servant does not know his master's business. Instead, I have called you friends, for everything that I learned from my Father I have made known to you.
John 15:12-15.

Jesus is their Lord and Master who teaches them. They are disciples learning from him. Yet he shares with them in a way that makes them friends. He confides in them and shares openly what God had given him. He poured into their ear what the Father had placed on his heart.

This intimate friendship was not confined to Jesus' last hours, nor contained to only his closest disciples. It was much more generous than this. He was known as the friend of sinners. (Matthew 11:19). He had earned himself a nickname.

Nicknames tend to be revealing. My nickname on the football pitch 'chopper' lets you know I was a defensive midfielder of determined nature and limited ability, not a prolific and talented striker. Also my nickname, 'Bobo', after the clown, will tell you how my biology teacher sought to redeem my messing about and distracting others in class. Sometimes nicknames are not so straightforward, there are those ironically dubbed, 'Tiny' who are anything but. They may also sometimes be randomly assigned, as for a friend who once ordered a burger in a chipper (Irish chip shop) and has been known as 'Burgers' from then on.

Jesus earned his nickname. 'Friend of sinners' fitted him well. This is the shape of Jesus' life as we encounter him in the Gospels (the four books that tell his story from the perspective of eyewitnesses). Luke, especially, has an emphasis on how Jesus extends friendship to outsiders. Whilst sharing the table with friends of a tax collector,

Jesus is the one extending hospitality to sinners through his friendship. It is gladly received, but the religious aren't enjoying the party. They are perplexed.

> "Why do you eat and drink with tax collectors and sinners?"Jesus answered them, "It is not the healthy who need a doctor, but the sick. I have not come to call the righteous, but sinners to repentance."
> Luke 5:30-32.

He is like a doctor coming to put sinners on a path to recovery and wellness, as he has come to call them to repentance, rather than the righteous. It seems Jesus' friendship was good news for sinners. In fact they seemed very comfortable and at ease in his presence. It was the religious who were disturbed. His friendship offered hope for those who were looked down on and held at arm's length by the society of their day. He wasn't so cold, rather his friendship extended an embrace.

This kind of friendship is not only hopeful, but also transformative. Further on in Luke's gospel, we meet another tax collector befriended by Jesus. Zacchaeus is so desperate to see Jesus he climbs a tree for a better view. The irony is that Jesus is looking for him.

When Jesus reached the spot, he looked up and said to him,

> "Zacchaeus, come down immediately. I must stay at your house today." So he came down at once and welcomed him gladly. All the people saw this and began to mutter, "He has gone to be the guest of a sinner."
> Luke 19:5-7.

Zacchaeus was a tax collector, classed by many Jews of the time as a traitor, working for the Romans against God's people, and also likely to be taking money for himself. He would have been short on friends. Yet, Jesus befriends him. In fact, he invites himself over to eat with him, which may sound impolite to our ears. You don't invite yourself over to someone else's home for food. The sad truth is it wouldn't even have entered Zacchaeus' mind to extend such an offer. He probably felt unworthy of receiving Jesus at his home. It may well seem that Zacchaeus welcomes Jesus gladly, but really it is Jesus who is befriending him. This friendship is deeply transformative, as he gives half of his possessions to the poor, and pays back those he had cheated four times. Such friendship is extended to us still.

In pursuit of friendship

Such deep friendships are precious enough to slow down and savour. It takes time to build such trust and closeness. Maybe even more costly, it takes a vulnerability to share precious hopes and fears and to allow another to come close.

In my journey of rest and recovery, graciously I'd been given another chance to develop such friendships.

In the summer of 2015 we had gone on holidays exhausted and looking for a way to keep going if we were to keep on serving with church. Through a time of rest and reflection there were two clear priorities and patterns I felt I was to establish:

1. to go slower and deeper with God

2. to share life with others by investing in genuine friendships.

It may sound somewhat strange to you that someone who is working as a pastor in a Christian church might need to learn to walk in these ways. Isn't being connected deeply to God and to others what it's all about? Well, yes, you'd have a point.

Yet in our busyness and work, we can all too easily lose sight of this. In working for God we can lose sight of God himself. We are more focused on the work of our hands than on his hand. So too with friendships. Very subtly people in Christian leadership may think they are the one ministering to others, being a friend to those in need, and yet failing to build genuine friendships themselves. This can be down to well-meaning care for others, or to focusing on plans and projects more than people. On reflection I recognised I had allowed my work to become a place where I would hide from being vulnerable. To be known, we need to share ourselves with others. This takes a courage I have to confess I too often lacked. It was much easier to keep a safe distance.

For those who are involved in leadership positions in work or church, let me acknowledge that these roles can come with more than their fair share of loneliness. Those who hold you in high esteem, and indeed those who do just the opposite, may keep a safe distance. Friendship is not extended. Let me suggest, however, all is not lost. Why not seek friendship with other leaders from outside your area of responsibility? If you reach out you could well find others who would value some support and encouragement. Perhaps if you're being honest, you might reflect and recognise that there are other reasons why you hide yourself from friendship with others.

In my period of recovery, my relational world had become smaller, whilst my longing for deep friendships had become greater. Through this time, reading Scripture and praying, a third priority was impressed on me

3. going deeper with fewer.

Our deepest friendships can begin in the most surprising of places. For some reading this book, it will sound strange to you to consider church as a community of friends.

Maybe your impression of church is one where the leader lectures the congregation on how they can live better. He is preaching from a pulpit on high, distanced from the people, far from the soul friend who draws alongside. Or maybe your experience of church is one of being lost in the crowd, no-one taking the time to get to know you. Perhaps most alarmingly of all in recent years, across various Christian traditions, stories have emerged of prominent leaders who misused their spiritual friendship with the most vulnerable and caused them great harm. If this is your impression of church I can understand why you'd keep your distance.

This impression, however, is some distance from the author and founder of the Christian Church, the friend of sinners. It is also far removed from the early church addressed in the New Testament Scriptures.

The dominant picture in the New Testament of the loving church community is of a family of brothers and sisters. At the end of the letter of 3 John we find such love described differently.

I hope to see you soon, and we will talk face to face.
Peace to you. The friends here send their greetings.
Greet the friends there by name.
3 John 14.

The people in the church are described as friends, those who love each other and lay down their lives for friends, just as Jesus did. They greet one another by name, a sign of being known personally and suggestive of a small community, in which people are recognised and cared for.

Such a community of people who know each other by name reminds me of the American sitcom Cheers. It was popular in the 1980s and featured a bar in Boston where an unlikely bunch of friends could go and share the highs and lows of their life with friends. It was a place of laughter and cheer. It was somewhere you could go where everybody knew your name, where you shared in your common humanity and struggles.

Such a longing, or place of belonging, captures well the friendship the apostle John has found in church. Here is the encouragement and challenge for those of you reading who belong to a church, to be such friends. Imagine what hope might be brought by people who are sincere and steadfast in their concern for others, who are close enough to listen and share words of comfort or challenge. Such people are good friends. They are safe people, worthy of trust.

They are people you'd love to see face to face. As John writes the letter to this church he is deliberately short. He prefers to see them soon and to talk face to face.

Here John alludes to a priority in terms of communication, of moving from the page to the person. Today we might suggest a similar hierarchy of communications from a text message or email, to an audio conversation, to a video conversation, to an in-person conversation face to face. Of course certain forms of communication suit certain purposes, but when it comes to deepening friendships, conversing together in person is the richest form of communication.

These days we tend to prefer connection to conversation. So suggests Sherry Turkle in her piece in the New York Times entitled, 'The Flight from Conversation.' She writes, "Human relationships are rich: they're messy and demanding. We have learned the habit of cleaning them up with technology."[5]

Could it be that we are hiding on Facebook or Instagram rather than meeting face to face with people? On social media we can maintain a safe distance. We can edit and project the image we'd like others to see rather than being honest about our failures and being vulnerable. In avoiding such time with others in person, we're shortchanging ourselves and also our friends.

Turkle suggests some habits she has developed which help keep certain spaces and times sacred and free from digital distractions, such as the dinner table, time in the car, or even catching up with friends. Such habits offer us hope in moving closer and deeper in our friendships.

However sometimes face to face can just feel too intense. I might suggest that a good place to start building friendship is to not focus on the other person 'head on' but rather to join in a shared passion, so that you might engage with one another side by side. Such support and friendship is the foundation of community groups for youth, or for parents and toddlers, or chatty cafes for those who are lonely, and is found in men's sheds and active retirement groups. Even something as simple as going for a walk with others can allow conversation to flow more freely and relationships to deepen and grow.

Finding friendship

Deep friendships, such as the soul friend of Celtic tradition, whilst hard to come by, are precious and worth investing in. With such friendships we might be known deeply in a world that is often only skimming the surface. With such trusted voices speaking hard words into our lives when we're losing our way, and tender ones when we've fallen, we are held steady in a culture being swept away by busyness. In an uncertain and turbulent world such deep human connections help us put down roots in wind and rain.

Let's hear the invitation to prize and pursue a few soul friends over many Facebook ones. Let's ask, not "How many friends do I have,' but rather, "How deep are my friendships?

Poems - The Garden Path & A Table for Three, by Seth Lewis.

These two poems capture two powerful skills that we already have that help us find friendship - walking and eating.[6]

The Garden Path

The best place for discussion
Is a pathway in a garden
For when our Maker made us
A garden's what he gave us
And when he came to speak with us
He walked along the path

A Table For Three

Sandwiches and
Cups of coffee
Two faces
Across from me
A wooden bench
A simple lunch
I rise to leave
I am
Nourished

Questions

1. Where might you be feeling the distance at the moment?
2. Thinking of someone who is a good friend, what qualities in them do you appreciate the most?
3. How might the description of Jesus as 'the friend of sinners' compare to your experience and understanding of church and Christian community?
4. What habits could you cultivate to prioritise friendship with others in person rather than on screen? What activity could you do side by side with others to deepen friendships?

Prayer

In a world of diverse distances - Lord we long for closeness,
and yet so often keep ourselves at a safe distance from you and others.
Friend of sinners, might you win over our hard hearts and suspicious souls, that we might find in you our true soul friend.
Might we offer such Jesus-like friendship to others
as well as being safe in the sweet embrace of such friendships ourselves.

CHAPTER THREE

RECOVERING MY BODY

Clay not Machine

**...for he knows how we are formed,
he remembers that we are dust.
Psalm 103:14**

Bodily conscious

When our bodies are healthy we don't think of them very often. We tend to tune out and forget what they may be saying to us. However somewhere along the way we encounter sickness, and they decide they deserve a little bit of attention and choose to say hello.

Following three months of lockdown we looked forward to holidays. All the adjustments to my life with pharmacy, church and home had taken their toll. It was time to lighten the load.

The first week was full of happy reunions with family and friends. Laughter and life shared together. Friendships that do the soul good. We breathed the fresh air of the great garden of the outdoors, walked in forests and waded through rivers, ran along roads and rested in gardens. The stuff that makes your soul sing.

The middle Saturday began in the happy company of a cup of coffee in one hand and a book in the other. This happiness was interrupted when I felt a dull and heavy ache at the back of my head, which spread across the top. I was accustomed to migraines as my warning sign of pushing myself too hard physically. Every now and again I had learned to pay attention to what they were saying and relieve the symptoms with medicine and rest. This pain however, felt different.

I stood up to get some medicine from the kitchen and nearly fell over. My arms and legs were wildly uncoordinated. Ally was in the room and as I chatted with her I felt some tingling in my arms. As we talked my tongue felt heavy and my words sounded a little slurred. I also felt dizzy. What kind of headache is this? Some strange neurological migraine like I've never had before? Or could it possibly be a stroke? We were naming the acronym FAST (Face, Arms, Speech, Time) out loud and managed to tick enough boxes to prompt Ally to ring for help.

A short time later the ambulance arrived and the paramedics assessed me. My vital signs were all stable but I was still unable to mobilise on my own. I was very dizzy, uncoordinated and feeling sick. So it was off along the twists and turns of back roads to the nearest hospital.

I arrived in the Emergency Department sick and thinking this is just a migraine. There was no cause for alarm. This mood seemed to match the staff around me. Something seemed to change however, as I was taken quickly into a CT scan. Shortly after I was informed I had a 2.3cm bleed on my brain around my cerebellum.

After another scan and discussions with neurosurgeons in Belfast, I was transferred to the Royal Victoria Hospital for further assessment and observation. As I arrived on the ward in Belfast I was being sick. I also felt dizzy, not in my head, but in my stomach. I can only compare it to the times when you go up or down on a rollercoaster, but more intense and coming without movement. I'd never felt anything like it and at the time didn't recognise it as dizziness.

I was glad to be in the hands of doctors and nurses who were assessing me, as well as radiologists who would see what was going on inside. It was only with their clinical skills and the scans that I was able to make sense of what my body was telling me before. The strange headache was the feeling of the bleed happening. Thankfully it stopped almost as soon as it started. The rest of the symptoms were the result of this. What had happened in a number of seconds would take my body months to recover fully from.

At the time my happiest place was with my eyes closed, my body still, and my breathing calm. I made my world small and still. This relieved the pressing symptoms of sickness and dizziness. I was brought to the present and more mindful of my body than ever before.

The attention given to my body helped silence a voice that had been in my head in the ambulance saying, "You've finally done it. Forty years old and you've had a stroke. You've finally broken yourself." I was all too conscious of my own tendency to overwork. I had come up against this trait of running myself into the ground too often in the past.

Over the coming weeks, as I recovered strength, my mind revisited the time before for any warning signs I may have missed. Despite no high blood pressure nor significant feelings of stress, I could recall moments where I felt I was pulling from a deep place within me. Had I become depleted deep beneath the surface? Just like aggressive farming might leach the soil of its goodness, I had done the same to my body. The comforts of sweet treats and increased amounts of caffeine, which were both trends in my coping with lockdown demands, were akin to reaching for fertiliser to stimulate the already depleted soil.

Bodily unconscious

In our current culture in the Western world we are all too unconscious of the demands we place on our bodies by how we are choosing to live. Most of us are prone to hurry and it is making us unwell. These were my thoughts in the hurried space of the pharmacy, in which I was surrounded by medicines to help the body. In one of our quieter moments, I recall a conversation with a colleague about how much our lifestyle affects nearly every aspect of our health. The medicines were arranged around us in categories laid out in the British National Formulary, which largely follow parts of the body. So, as we talked our way around the dispensary we moved from cardiac to mental health to stomach to pain to diabetes to reproductive health. In every one of these, stress and strain leave their mark.

It might seem a touch ironic that as we worked with medicines we were discussing our over-reliance on them, 'a pill for every ill' as they say. Now, I'm not going to renounce my training and confidence in medicines to improve our health, but I would suggest we have learned to rely too much on medicine and not pay enough attention to diet, exercise in the great outdoors, and time with good friends. Our healthcare has become more reactive than proactive. We are more focused on disease than on wellness and then only pay attention to our bodies when they trouble us.

Might it be that we are lost in our own heads or caught up so much in our own hurry that we have become disconnected from our own bodies? So we end up depleting them just as the soil is leached of nutrients.

Embodied souls

This connection between soil and our bodies is made in the biblical story. We are made of the same stuff. Let's take a walk back to the beginning in Eden garden again.

Then the Lord God formed a man from the dust of the ground and breathed into his nostrils the breath of life, and the man became a living being.
Genesis 2:7.

We are made of matter, the very dust of the ground. If your initial reaction is to object due to a difference in chemical composition between bodies and soil, then let me invite you to consider the poetic picture that is being offered to us. We are from the ground, yet by the breath of God we are given the kiss of life. We are a living being or soul or person. This is the consistent view of our humanity throughout the Bible, which describes human beings as embodied souls.[7]

Here is a lofty view of humanity. We are formed by the hands of a Creator who is a master craftsman. This is what the word "formed" in Genesis 2:7 means, we are shaped and crafted carefully. So that in the praise book of the Bible, King David exalts God.

> I praise you for I am fearfully and wonderfully made;
> your works are wonderful, I know that full well.
> Psalm 139:14.

Just as drinking in the beauty of a remarkable piece of pottery would cause us to appreciate the skill of the potter, there is something in us as humans made to reflect the beauty of our Creator. In the Christian worldview our dignity and worth are found in being created in the image of God.

We are also made of the earth. Here is a truth that grounds us and keeps us from losing our heads in the clouds. It lowers our loftiness. There is a beautiful balance to be found in the biblical view of humanity as embodied souls. In our bodies we are capable of connecting with our God and yet we have managed to forget ourselves and him.

Isaiah, as one of the prophets, called out to God's people to return and remember him. With many poetic pictures he pleaded with them. Including using the image of the potter and the clay.

> Yet you, LORD, are our Father.

We are the clay, you are the potter;
we are all the work of your hand.
Isaiah 64:8.

Could it be we have forgotten the Potter's hand and forgotten we are clay? We are in a rush to achieve and accomplish more and more in less and less time. We are sick with hurry. We have forgotten our limits. As clay we are more fragile, finite, and fleeting than we care to imagine or acknowledge.

There is much to be learned in the prayer of Psalm 90, attributed to Moses, a man of God.

Teach us to numbers our days,
that we may gain a heart of wisdom.
Psalm 90:12.

Not seizing the day. No, rather recognising our days are numbered. One day we will return to the dust from which we came. Maybe this sounds completely depressing? It takes the wind out of our sails. It certainly makes us more humble in our living. You may find it strange if I say I actually find this incredibly liberating. The truth that we are embodied souls, that we live with limits, reminds me that our worth is not found in our productivity or usefulness. We are clay and not machine.

Somewhere along the way we have become disconnected from our bodies. They are just the vehicle we travel in through life. So we might talk about ourselves as cars travelling along the road of life.

- When we're tired, "We're running on empty."
- If you're from certain parts of Ireland and things are going well, "You're sucking diesel."
- When we do things which energise us, "We're filling our tank."

Whilst we should not take these terms too seriously,

language is important. How we name things, influences how we understand them and may even become a self-fulfilling prophecy. Our words can create; we can become what they say. I can laugh off the 'sucking diesel' comment, but there is something about 'filling our tank' that grates on me. Maybe it's because I've heard it used to try and bring help to those who are on the brink of burn out. They need to be more mindful of activities in their lives that feed their souls rather than drain their energy. So they need to fill their tanks. Yet to me, it is more fitting to use language that issues from the ground for just such times. We are more like grass that flourishes and fades than cars which rust and decay. We are living beings.

Maybe the language of machines grates on me because it hits close to home. My body longs to be treated like clay, yet too often I have put it to work like a machine. It is handed over to do the bidding of the many ideas and strong desires that stir inside. I have in some way lost touch with my own body. I have become disconnected and fragmented within myself, as I have become disconnected from the Bible's insight that I am an embodied soul. I have been distanced from the hands of my Creator and have lived as though the power to change lies in my hands alone.

Embodied God

There is good news however, as this distance *from* God has been covered *by* God. He has come near. At the beginning of John's gospel we are introduced to the Word, who we learn is God and was with God in the beginning. (John 1:1-18). He was fully involved and instrumental in creation and yet the wonder is that he makes his home in this creation, as he inhabits a human body. He is truly God and also truly human, and so an embodied soul.

In lowering himself he has given us an even higher view of humanity. The Embodied God dignifies our bodies. He understands our embodied humanity, meeting our deepest needs to be known and understood. He came to restore and free our mortal bodies. He shared our humanity, so that in living and then tasting death, Jesus has freed us from death and its fear (Hebrews 2:14-15).

The Christian worldview presents a new creation that will come in which our bodies are liberated from death and decay. This hope is not for some disembodied spirit floating in heavenly clouds. Rather it is, as we read in chapter 1 of this book, savouring the garden of the new heaven and new earth, with real bodies. Bodies that the apostle Paul says are no longer weak or diseased but healthy and strong. Immortal.

> When the perishable has been clothed with the imperishable, and the mortal with immortality, then the saying that is written will come true, "Death has been swallowed up in victory."
> 1 Corinthians 15:54.

This hope of actual bodily immortality is in the future. For now, however, our bodies have limits. In light of this, the apostle Paul speaks of Christians as jars of clay who have a great treasure within.

> But we have this treasure in jars of clay to show that this all-surpassing power is from God and not from us. We are hard pressed on every side, but not crushed; perplexed, but not in despair; persecuted, but not abandoned; struck down, but not destroyed. We always carry around in our body the death of Jesus, so that the life of Jesus may also be revealed in our body.
> 2 Corinthians 4:7-10.

Clay jars were pretty ordinary and commonplace in the time and place Paul lived. They were also fragile and needed to be handled with care. Here is the humbling reminder that I am weaker than I would ever care to admit. The treasure within is the power and life of Jesus who lives in us. Our challenges and weakness are the way

Christians carry around his death and also display his life as we depend on him. Our bodies are where he has chosen to make his home. God is embodied in us, as the Holy Spirit lives in us. His treasure in our jars of clay.

Being kind to the clay - Sabbath rest

As clay we all live with limits. This has been one of the greatest lessons I've learned in my recovery. My energy from day to day was unpredictable and limited. I had to pay attention to it and make choices on how to spend it. In the earliest days, I had to choose the moments and ways I could spend time with my family and when I needed to rest. In more recent days I pay attention to when I am more irritable or strained and show signs of tiredness. I am more conscious and even curious as to how my body is doing on a day to day basis.

As I write I have recovered well from my bleed, and also from surgery which removed an AVM (arteriovenous malformation), a tangle of weak blood vessels which needed to be addressed to prevent a rebleed. My journeys of recovery in past years mean I am more conscious of my body and have learned to take better care of myself.

I am glad I have learned that my body has limited resources, just like my bank account, so I'd be wise to choose well how I spend it. Just like my finances, when I am overdrawn, my body suffers the penalties.

When we live more like machine than clay, we are refusing ourselves the kindness of rest and recuperation. A farmer who depletes the soil of nutrients may reap a more immediate and increased harvest by the use of artificial fertilisers, but he will pay in the long-term. His harshness has leached the land of life.

In the Old Testament, God's people were commanded to take care of the land by allowing it to rest every seven years. Just as they were to rest every seven days on the Sabbath, so the land enjoyed a sabbatical, to rest and recover. (Leviticus 25:1-7).

In the early days of lockdowns there was some degree

of decrease in commuting and pollution. The question was therefore being asked, "Could this rest do our environment good?" Maybe for you the interruption of hurried lives and work schedules led to a welcome sabbatical. A chance to rest and recover. Or possibly the increased demands of work, family, and life in a time of Covid left you weary. Or, as you read now, you would love some time to rest, as the ongoing demands of life have drained you. If ever you needed a sabbatical, it is now.

Despite learning to go slower and deeper and having intentional rhythms in place to rest and recharge, I had been putting off the need to take an extended holiday or sabbatical. It just wasn't the right time for it. The church needed me too much (a foolish notion that was disposed of in how well they fared during my absence). In my time of rest and recovery I reflected and concluded that I had been on the road too long and asking too much of myself. Now I was being graciously invited to rest and recover. In some ways I was enjoying a type of sabbatical.

I viewed this as God's kindness to me. Even previous to my bleed, I had written rhythms of rest into my daily, weekly, and even yearly routines, to which I tried to hold.

- My days began with a slow time to pray and reflect on the Bible, and would continue with margins especially around mealtimes to stop and breathe in the day's busyness.
- My weeks included family night on Fridays with homemade pizza and a movie or games. This continued with time together on our family day off until Saturday evening. In addition to this there was a quiet morning in the middle of the week, which could include reading or time walking or biking outdoors.
- My years would include times for holidays mainly in the summer, but also at Easter and Christmas. I learned not to work against the grain or to push hard when others were slowing to stop.

Now I was being invited to go beyond these habits and to rest for longer. In writing rhythms of rest across our lives we are taking good care of the bodies God has given us. In encouraging others and giving them permission toward the same rest we are showing them kindness.

So it was in my rest and recovery. I was in the company of those who gave me the space and time needed to recover. When I was restored to health and strong enough to return, and was cleared to do so by my doctor, I enjoyed the kindness of a chorus of voices encouraging me to take it easy and find my feet again gradually. For this community of kindness I am deeply grateful. I wasn't a machine that needed to be more productive and get back to work. I was a human being, an embodied soul, made of clay and with treasure within, being supported towards recovery.

Such kindness reflects the heart of the one who made us embodied souls. The Father who has compassion on his children, as he knows our frame and remembers we are dust (Psalm 103:13-14). He is kind to the clay.

We are clay not machines, and so our bodies need to be handled with care as we make our way through life. As we connect and are more conscious of our bodies, especially in times of weakness, hear the invitation to take care of yourself and to find rest in placing yourself in the Potter's hands.

As complex and contradictory human beings, let's also pay attention to how we might lovingly encourage others to take good care of themselves, but which we might all too often neglect to do for our own bodies.

Poem - Go gently

Go gently into the light of day,
Welcome easy graces along the stony path.
Fruitful work and thorny strife fill hands and day,
Till evening's rest receives us home at last.
Aching bones slow and sit and fall to bed
and rise refreshed to go again.

Questions

1. What signs of hurry sickness do you see in your own life or those around you?
2. When might you have shown signs of living like a machine rather than as clay?
3. In what ways might your weaknesses be a way of showing God's treasure in your life?
4. What or who encourages you to take good care of yourself and to practice regular rhythms of rest?
5. In what ways might you intentionally build rest or stops into your life?

Prayer

You are the Potter, we are the clay.

Lord, might you grow in us an understanding of the beautiful balance of being embodied souls, made to show your beauty in our weakness.

Thank you Jesus that you are the Word made flesh, who came to live and die and rise that you might make your home in us.

Help us show kindness to ourselves and to others
Knowing our frame, remembering we are of dust.

CHAPTER FOUR

RECOVERING OUR HEARTS

My heart is faint

I thirst for you like a parched land
Psalm 143:6b

The O'Donovan brothers from Skibbereen shone brightly
in the summer of 2016. Smiles beamed from the faces of
many who made their acquaintance. At the Rio Olympics
the rowers' easy-going, good-natured humour was a breath
of fresh air. Increasingly, interviews with sportspeople are
akin to squeezing water from a stone. Give nothing away.
Paul and Gary O'Donovan were about as far from this as
you could possibly get. They were refreshingly
themselves. Their 'Wesht' Cork accents and humour
endeared them to many beyond their native Ireland.

This humour flowed freely even in the midst of the
high pressure and high performance environment of the
Olympics. They seemed to be carrying the pressure well.
Those who misjudged them as a couple of easy going
Irishmen - there just to take part - would find the last
laugh was on them. The brothers returned home with
silver medals.

They seemed to be gliding through the water as they
raced. Flowing freely. Under the surface, however, it took

the endurance and energy to work to 90% of output for around seven minutes. Most of us would tire rapidly under such heavy loads, but they had endured the rigorous training needed to ensure they could carry it well. All this meant they could "Close their eyes and pull like a dog," as Paul O'Donovan famously put it.

My heart is faint

We've been working hard ourselves over the past few years, making our way through Covid and out the other side. We've become all too familiar with bearing the heavy loads of our emotions. Is it any wonder at times along the way we were feeling faint? We've been carrying the weight of grief for a prolonged period. Never mind the considerable burden of anxiety that accompanied each twist and turn. This is to name but two of the myriad of emotions making turbulent waters under the surface. Life is a mysterious medley of messy emotions at the best of times, but when we face trying times we find ourselves more shaken and stirred than ever before.

My heart is faint. The words resonated with me as I led our church family in a time of praying through a selection of Psalms, which helped us call out to God from a messy myriad of emotions. We were responding not only to Covid, but also the aftershocks of the earthquake that followed the death of George Floyd, which had travelled across the Atlantic and had deeply shaken those in our own multicultural church family. There was pain, hurt, and grief from those who were black and identified strongly with this trauma, and felt it deeply. Sadly, some of us from other ethnicities were slow to stand in solidarity and sympathy. As I was leading others, I too was feeling faint.

My heart had been working hard not only with the weight of Covid and racial justice, but also with reading and reflecting on the troubled history of the island of Ireland. I'd also been naming and lamenting the persistent indifference, and growing hostility, of many in Ireland today to the good news of the Jesus I loved. I was also walking alongside others as a pastor in their brokenness and difficulty. My journal was full, as I had been naming these feelings and handing them over, and so I went on holidays feeling light. But my heart had been worked hard.

I'll never know how much a part this all played in the bleed on my brain. Did some of the stress I was under and the faintness I felt contribute to my stroke? The medics assured me that risk factors, including high blood pressure or being a smoker, were more significant and reassuringly absent in my case. One of the doctors however, was honest enough to remind me of the complexity of our brains and how so much could be happening under the surface. So, whilst not the direct cause, faintness of heart was part of the presenting environment.

Finding our flow

What might we do with our emotions then? The current wisdom is to name our feelings and accept them. To resist them or work against them is to cause ourselves harm. So the best thing to do with grief is to allow yourself to feel it and keep going. We are to watch our emotions as they pass. To let them flow through us as we move along.[8]

I find these ideas of recognising emotions as they move through us, and not judging ourselves too quickly for how we feel, to be helpful. However this is also particularly elusive, as if we might somehow detach ourselves and become a spectator, when our feelings are an intricate part of who we are. I also think this view implies we are passengers to our feelings, whilst the Bible generously gives us words for them that might shape them as they flow through us.

It is interesting however, that such liquid language is used of our heart in the Bible, underlining its central role in who we are.

Above all else, guard your heart,
 for everything you do flows from it.
Proverbs 4:23.

In the Bible, the heart represents the inner person: thinkings and feelings, which lead to our doings. It is the fountain from which our very life flows. We are to pay attention to it and be vigilant, naming those feelings.

 Many people today find mindfulness exercises helpful to keep in touch with their feelings and thoughts, and to pay attention to them as they move through us. There are a wide range of different understandings and practices of meditation. These include the attempt to empty ourselves to find calm or even to open ourselves to spirits as in some Eastern traditions, or just the opposite in Christian traditions, where the mind might be filled with truths which we then contemplate. As I write from a Christian viewpoint it will be no surprise that I have serious concerns about the former and find safe ground in the latter. What I have in mind however, when I write about mindfulness, is the idea of certain breathing exercises that help us slow down and tune in to our own bodies, including our thoughts and feelings. Such exercises are a help to many as our lives are far from flowing, but rather full of distractions and interruptions.

During Covid times we were displaced from our normal rhythms and routines. On numerous occasions we were interrupted, or faced multiple unexpected changes. This contributed to a feeling of languishing, which was recognised as a feeling of stagnation or emptiness.[9] One of the suggested antidotes to this languishing is to find something that we might love doing so much that we lose ourselves in it, to find a flow to life.

I wonder if these distractions and interruptions grew from seeds sown before Covid rained on the world and caused them to grow? Could it be that snacking on social media, being immersed in our phones, being continually interrupted by messages has left us malnourished?

Of course there are positives in digital communication and technology, like smartphones. There is, however, something iconic about our engagement with our phones. They are more than just one of numerous examples of distraction and are rather representative of the age we live in. It is a metaphor for how we do life these days. In scrolling our feeds, we've neglected to feed our souls. In skimming and skipping from one app to the next, we lack any depth. We find ourselves empty. Languishing.

The causes of our languishing lie *before* Covid came and also lie *beneath* the skimming on the surface of life. Our hearts are thirsting for something deeper. Technology is only one of the fountains from which we choose to drink to quench our thirst for life.

Finding fulfilment

He was dying of thirst, surrounded by water, but unable to drink it. It was Spring 1943. American soldier, Louis Zamperini, was floating in the Pacific Ocean with sharks underneath and Japanese planes seeking him from above and yet, his thirst was his greatest enemy. Zamperini was a runner at the 1936 Berlin Olympics. His athletic strength and discipline were being sorely tested now. If he drank the saltwater he would become even more severely dehydrated. He survived for an amazing 47 days and lived to tell the tale.

Whilst we may not be afloat at sea, this thirst is something we all have and yet we find it all too easy to reach for the saltwater. This not only fails to satisfy us, it makes us even more thirsty. What is this saltwater? I have already suggested it could be technology. It could just as easily be money, sex, work, or family. The saltwater is what the Bible describes as idols. They are good things that we turn into god things. Anything that we look to instead of God to meet our deepest thirst for life. When we worship idols, we drink saltwater, but God invites us to come to him and drink.[10]

53

As Covid interrupted our world, I was finding I needed to go deeper. I found my own sense of flow in spending more time delighting in the Bible. I was noticing my mood, speech, and actions were increasingly strained and so I needed more time in prayer, soaking in the Psalms. This book in the Scriptures is the prayer book of believers and has been a solace to many in times of trouble down through history. In 1557 John Calvin wrote, "I have been accustomed to call this book...An Anatomy of the Soul; for there is not an emotion of which anyone can be conscious that is not here represented as in a mirror."[11]

The Psalms give words to our feelings which we name before God. So they follow the same path as the mindfulness practices as I described them before, yet with a key difference; God is in the picture. We are not talking to ourselves, but involving him in the conversation.

At the doorway to this Bible book, in its opening Psalm, we find a picture that is a tonic to those whose hearts are faint. If in languishing we feel so far from thriving in life we might lose hope of ever finding our way, here is comfort. For the one who meditates on God's words day and night, who prayerfully soaks their minds and hearts in these Psalms, they are:

> like a tree planted by streams of water,
> which yields its fruit in season
> and whose leaf does not wither.
> Psalm 1:3.

Here is an invitation to dwell deeply on words which will water our thirsty souls. To put down roots. This will give strength and stability when the storms and stresses of life come our way. It will also nourish us just as the roots of a tree draw up nutrients from the ground in which they are planted. They drink in life from the streams of water that are God's words of life.

Mindfulness and breathing exercises can be helpful practices in dealing with the surface level emotions flowing through us. Here is a much bolder claim; that our deepest thoughts and emotions can be shaped by these living words we read. We can find depth that addresses the source of them - the heart - which is the spring and fountain of life.

As we have seen in chapters 1-3 of this book, we have deep rifts between ourselves and nature, our friendships, our bodies, and even God himself. We enter by the Psalms into the wisdom literature of the Scriptures, where we also find the books called Proverbs, Ecclesiastes and Job. We will seek, over the next few chapters, to put down roots in these precious words of wisdom, to find life that is heart deep and which overflows into our work, our seasons, and our sufferings; our whole lives.

For now we will stay in the Psalms. If Psalm 1 is a doorway to this prayer book, which invites us to go deeper into life, then the closing Psalm 150 is the fulfilment of the pathway made in prayer that brings us to the heights. It is written in the language of free flowing song and dance. Like crashing waves there are noisy cymbals and a swell of praise to God. There is nothing tentative or timid about this celebration. It is a free flowing party of praise; everything that has breath is invited. Here is life fulfilled.

> Praise the Lord.
> Praise God in his sanctuary;
> praise him in his mighty heavens.
> Praise him for his acts of power;
> praise him for his surpassing greatness.
> Praise him with the sounding of the trumpet,
> praise him with the harp and lyre,
> praise him with timbrel and dancing,
> praise him with the strings and pipe,
> praise him with the clash of cymbals,
> praise him with resounding cymbals.
> Let everything that has breath praise the Lord.
> Praise the Lord.
> Psalm 150

Words for our feelings

This free flowing song and dance may feel sorely detached from your present reality. It is disconnected from the weariness from the weight of emotions I expressed at the start of this chapter. How is this helpful? Isn't it cruel to expect such praise in a world filled with very real sorrow? Such a response might flow from a view of God that has been passed on to you, that he is high and lofty, demanding and expecting too much of us.

If this is the case, the path from the first Psalm to the last might surprise you. Every emotion is provided for, yet the majority are laments. They are written to help us with our grief and loss in a broken and suffering world. They offer us a way of handing our sorrows over to God. Some even give us words for the loss of God himself, for when we feel God-abandoned. So, it is in God's grace that he has gifted us with words for when we most feel his absence. We can allow God's words to address our feelings, but the Bible, God's word, also gives us words to bring our feelings to God.

While we might like to let our emotions flow through us, there are times when we feel like we're drowning in them. Our hearts are swirling with thoughts and emotions which we find hard to describe or understand. For this, God has graciously gifted us words to find our way, which are like footholds when all around is fluid.

These Psalms of lament, which help us express sorrow and frustration, include Psalm 42. The words we are given come from the deep waters of our emotions. There are tears day and night, a pouring out of soul, and a 'deep calling to deep' in the roar of waterfalls. They are drowning in their sorrows, as they talk to themselves.

> Why, my soul, are you downcast?
> Why are you so disturbed within me?
> Put your hope in God, for I will yet praise him,
> my Saviour and my God.
> Psalm 42:5, 11.

These words are repeated twice, in the middle of the Psalm and at its end. They are a foothold and the firmest ground we have in the watery words. There is an honesty about feeling down and disturbed, but yet a hope that this will pass. What might sound at first confused or contradictory, is actually a conversation. This is the tension the language of lament allows for. Psalms of lament enable people who trust in God to name the sadness of harsh realities, whilst holding on to the one who loves them through it all.

The Irish are no strangers to sadness. This is the hard-learned lesson of repeated hardship and suffering. The sadness of our long history has left its mark. Across the years we've found words that have helped us lament through stories and poems and songs. It is striking that one of the most passionate of current anthems sung out by Irish crowds supporting soccer and rugby teams, is actually a lament. The Fields of Athenry was written relatively recently, in 1979, yet it is in a long line of folk songs written from the pain of emigration and the Irish potato famine (1845-1852).

So it could be that sadness is written into our national DNA. In Ireland, however, we know everything about being complex and contradictory. As we faced the grief of the Covid pandemic we heard the call ring out more than ever to stay positive. We were encouraged to practise being grateful and name our blessings in life. The book of Psalms again presents us with the words to bring thanks and praise to God. Yet I worry that this cultural call removes permission to lament. It doesn't allow for singing a different song or praying a different prayer. In only focusing on the positive, what happens to our feelings of frustration or grief that lie beneath the surface?

In recent years there has been an active movement towards being more open about how we feel. The stigma that has been associated with mental health conditions has been reduced. "It's ok not to feel ok, and it's absolutely ok to ask for help." The listening ear of a trusted friend, or maybe even the help of a trained counsellor can be invaluable. I wonder though, if our reputation for resilience works against this?

The trait of resilience has been issued as a rallying cry on more than one occasion in speeches to the nation over testing times in recent years. It's something we're known for. Could it be that it might inhibit us from complaining too much? How many times have we said, "someone else has it worse than me?" Are we reluctant to lament and give words to our feelings?

The trait of resilience was deeply etched on the life of Louis Zamperini. He survived the ocean and then endured two different Japanese prisoner of war camps. Since he was a famous American athlete, they tried to break his strength. To make an example of him. One commander called 'The Bird' was particularly cruel to him.

In the film, 'Unbroken', which tells Louis' life story, is a central scene that shows him at his lowest point, tired and injured.[12] He is told to lift a large steel beam above his head. If he drops it the guards are to shoot him. The whole camp watches on. Defiantly he holds it above his head for hours until nightfall. He will not be broken. He was strong both physically and mentally.

Such trauma left its scars. Back home after the war he was haunted by nightmares of The Bird beating him. He suffered from Post Traumatic Stress Disorder. The strong man mentality that had helped him survive, was now breaking him. He was too strong to ask for help. He eased the pain with alcohol. He picked fights. He was on the brink of divorce. Broken.

Feeling with us

Jesus was no stranger to brokenness and weakness, yet he chose to face it differently. He turned to his Father in need of help. In Luke's gospel we read of how he regularly sought strength in prayer.

But Jesus often withdrew to lonely places and prayed. Luke 5:16.

As the cross appeared on the horizon, he often sought his Father in prayer (Luke 3:21-22, 5:15-16, 6:12-13, 9:18, 22:40-46).

Supremely, as he suffered the anguish of the cross, he continued to cry out to his Father using the words of Psalm 22, a Psalm of lament.

My God, my God why have you forsaken me?
Why are you so far from saving me, so far from my cries of anguish?
My God, I cry out by day, but you do not answer,
by night but I find no rest.
Psalm 22:1-2.

In the Christian story the most powerful permission to lament is given by the perfect Son of God, crying out on the cross. As God's perfect Son, he is the model human being who, in his suffering, calls out with the words of this lament.

So, as we encounter the words of lament in the Psalms, we know he prays them with us. In his humanity he feels with us. He understands all our emotions. We can freely hand them over to Him.

Forsaken for us

Jesus not only feels with us, but was forsaken for us. His calling out in his abandonment is called the cry of dereliction. He is God-forsaken. In this he fulfilled Psalm 22 which contains many allusions to the crucifixion, yet was written hundreds of years previously.

I am poured out like water and all my bones are out of joint.
My heart has turned to wax; it has melted within me.
My mouth is dried up like a potsherd,

and my tongue sticks to the roof of my mouth;
you lay me in the dust of death.
Psalm 22:14-15.

This idea of fulfilment is found not only at the cross,
but also at the beginning and end of Luke's account of
Jesus' life; on the first page and also the last. He opens by
introducing his account of what has been fulfilled or
accomplished through Jesus.

Many have undertaken to draw up an account of the
things, "...that has been fulfilled among us..." (Luke 1:1).

Throughout its pages, Luke unfolds the theme of
God's plan of salvation in history being fulfilled in Jesus.
Finally, at the end of the gospel, following his death and
resurrection, Jesus assures his disciples,

This is what I told you while I was still with you:
everything must be fulfilled that is written about me
in the Law of Moses, the Prophets and Psalms.
Luke 24:44.

Jesus was forsaken to fulfil God's plan of salvation for
a world ravaged by sin, which still leaves its mark on the
depths of our sorrowful and thirsty hearts. The hope for
faint hearts is found in him. He is the one who satisfies
our deepest spiritual thirst. As Jesus hangs on the cross,
another Psalm of lament is on his lips, as he says, "I am
thirsty" (John 19:28, alluding to Psalm 69:21). He does
this "so that Scripture would be fulfilled". In suffering
thirst, Jesus brings us the deepest refreshment and
satisfaction. In dying he brings us life, as his forsakenness
brings fulfilment. So we can freely hand over our sorrows
and our sin to him, knowing he suffered for us.

This message of the cross was heard by Louis
Zamperini as his wife took him to hear the famous
preacher Billy Graham. In his brokenness and at his
weakest, he came to find strength in God. To quench his
deepest thirst.

Here is life for the languishing. We can name all our emotions before the one who feels with us and who was forsaken for us. We can cycle through the prayers of the Psalms in all our changing emotions. We can pour out our hearts to him, finding our flow when our hearts are faint. We can drink deeply from the fountain of life.

Poem - Psalm 42:1-5

As the deer pants for streams of water,
    so my soul pants for you, my God.
My soul thirsts for God, for the living God.
    When can I go and meet with God?
My tears have been my food
    day and night,
while people say to me all day long,
    "Where is your God?"
These things I remember
    as I pour out my soul:
how I used to go to the house of God
    under the protection of the Mighty One
with shouts of joy and praise
    among the festive throng.
Why, my soul, are you downcast?
    Why so disturbed within me?
Put your hope in God,
    for I will yet praise him,
    my Saviour and my God.

Questions

1. What feelings do you think we have been carrying as we recover from testing times as a society? What may have been weighing on your own heart?
2. What might be some of the common ways today in which we 'sip saltwater' to quench our spiritual thirst?
3. How does the picture of Jesus as a human who suffers, laments, and prays, fit with your understanding of him?
4. In what ways could you make a pattern of praying through the Psalms or the Scriptures?

Prayer

Lord God, we come to you with our faint and heavy hearts.

In our loss and sadness we come to the Father and the Son who have both known loss in the forsakenness of the cross.

Might you pour comfort into our hearts by the Holy Spirit,

as we pour out our hearts in prayer to you.

Might you quench our deepest thirst and satisfy us with your life

We hope in you for we will yet praise you, our Saviour and our God.

CHAPTER FIVE

RECOVERING OUR BALANCE

Finding our feet in an unsteady world

**Give careful thought to the paths for your feet
and be steadfast in all your ways.
Proverbs 4:26**

In search of balance

One man's walk between two towers captured the imagination and adulation of the world. On August 7 1974, high wire walker, Philippe Petit walked between the Twin Towers of the World Trade Centre in New York. With no safety net he was 1350 feet above the ground. He not only walked the 131 feet across the steel cable, but also lay down, saluted the sky and was in conversation with the birds. Although unannounced and seemingly spontaneous, such a high wire act took six years of planning and considerable practice. The craft of this work of art required consistent graft behind the scenes.[13]

Finding balance in our lives these days can feel just as challenging, but much less inspiring. Managing the busyness in our lives is like balancing on a high wire. So we walk carefully, acutely aware of the consequences should we fail and fall. We need to find a better work life balance. If someone would only tell us how to make this happen! Then, just when you're stretched and straining, the wind picks up. Life happens. Whether on a personal or global scale we can be shaken by winds of change that inevitably come our way.

The arrival of Covid shook our world. Amidst the storm we were not all in the same boat, but we shared the same conditions, as we found ourselves, 'all at sea.' Whatever our circumstances we were all trying to find our feet. As I considered the personal challenges that lay ahead, for our family and the church I serve, the question front and centre was, "How can we still be standing when this all passes?"

Finding my feet

When I suffered my bleed on the brain my balance was tested in a more significant, and very literal, way. The damage occurred around my cerebellum, the centre for balance and coordination. So recovery would involve searching for balance to find my feet again.

I got off to a shaky start. As I moved from lying to sitting to walking, I was initially assessed to need the assistance of a nurse or health care assistant. I was tentatively travelling in the company of a student nurse, when suddenly I lost balance and nearly went down in a heap. This shook not only my confidence, but that of the nurse too! It took the wisdom of a more mature and, let's say assertive, nurse to keep me from settling in my insecurity. She ordered me out of the chair and across the floor. The prospect of falling seemed less risky than disobeying orders!

I laughed with the physio as I acknowledged balance was never my strong suit. As mentioned before I was 'chopper' on the football pitch, more often on my backside sliding into challenges than beautifully weaving my way down the wing! Balletic I was not. The physio assured me that to gain my balance again I would need to challenge it. I was being extended away from my centre of gravity to help me grow stronger. It seemed there would be some more near misses ahead on the road to recovering balance.

Being top heavy

Finding our feet when Covid shook our world was a challenge. We were under pressure, as we struggled to keep up to date with information on the progress of the virus, how to keep ourselves safe and the updates to restrictions. The waves of cases seemed to have been matched by waves of information and anxiety. It all threatened to overwhelm us.

We were already swimming in information. We have instant inroads to information on anything we need to know at the touch of a button. Just ask Google or watch a short Youtube video to learn the latest skill we need. Never mind the constant news cycles and updates. I wonder if we were swept to sea because we chose to swim rather than stand? Were we tempted to take in more information rather than make some decisions and put them into practice? For all the data at our fingertips, are we any the wiser?

I remember feeling weary from the number of decisions to be made and also aware like never before that I was not in control. We love to make plans, but they were all washed away, offering us a clearer vision of how the world really is. It is always unsafe and uncertain. So as we make our way, we look for security. When we look in the wrong places, this only unsteadies us all the more.

My health recovery found me in a similar search for wisdom in recovering. Yet I too often relied on plans to control my environment and make it a safe space for me. My anxieties and uncertainties led to over-assessing, over-talking, and over-worrying. I just couldn't get my head around it all. My thinking was only making me dizzy.

In the West we continue to be influenced by the motto implanted in our minds by René Descartes, 'I think therefore I am.' The French philosopher and pioneering scientist lived from 1596-1650 and was a key influence in the philosophical revolution known as the Enlightenment, which began in the late seventeenth century. The focus on our ability to reason things out for ourselves, continues to leave its mark. I wonder if, like some strange sci-fi movie, we're moving around with gigantic heads, falling over and knocking one another over. Big brains but tiny hearts and hands. Alien to our humanity. We are top-heavy.

Balanced wisdom

A more balanced wisdom can be found in the biblical book of Proverbs which helps us find our feet on the path of life. This book explains that, the imbalanced view of the world that has no place for God, is shaky under our feet. It is the way of foolishness. We live without God in the picture, doing our own thing. With all our information and knowledge, we are wise in our own eyes. The result is an unsteadied and insecure existence. A way that will be exposed when stormy times come.

> Do you see a person wise in their own eyes?
> There is more hope for a fool than for them.
> Proverbs 26:12.

The contrasting path is the way of wisdom. When it is prized and sought after, there is a beauty to life and also safety. It is no guarantee to a trouble-free life, but rather a sure way of living freely in the midst of trouble. This is to live in a way that is true to the world, to others, to ourselves, and also to the one who made it. To live before his face and under his watch is the key to wisdom. This is captured in the phrase 'fear of the Lord'. To live like this is to find our feet. Here is wisdom that works. This way of life is shown strong when storms come.

> Whoever fears the Lord has a secure fortress,
> and for their children it will be a refuge.
> Proverbs 14:26.

The fear of the Lord is the beginning of wisdom. This is a strong and repeated theme through the book of Proverbs. For those who fear the Lord find they have nothing else to fear. Such fear may conjure in our minds the idea of dread or terror in the hands of an almighty God. While some of this might be involved in the phrase it might be better understood as awe or reverence as we recognise who he is and who we are not. He is God. We are not. So, he is not us. Indeed, in some measure, God is not safe in the sense that he does not answer to us or leave us unchallenged or unaccountable. Yet there is no safer place to be than with the one who is not safe. The God we should fear.

So it is in orienting ourselves to his ways that we have the surest and safest grounds to stand on. After all, he is himself a refuge.

> The name of the LORD is a fortified tower;
> the righteous run to it and are safe.
> Proverbs 18:10.

Such wisdom is found in Jesus' teaching. This is an especially prominent theme running through Matthew's Gospel. At the start of Jesus' ministry he calls people to "Repent, for the kingdom of heaven is at hand" (Matthew 4.17). This repentance calls for practical obedience based on a reorientation toward God and away from ourselves. It is, in fact, a rebalancing of our lives to his righteousness, described in his teaching. As Jesus gathers his disciples, the first major block of teaching in Matthew's Gospel is the Sermon on the Mount in chapters 5-7. He teaches them what it will look like to live in his Kingdom. Righteousness is a key word and theme. At the close of the Gospel, his teaching is what is to be passed on to people from all nations, as they become disciples and grow in their faith.

Much of Jesus' Sermon on the Mount resembles

wisdom literature. He closes the sermon with a picture of the wise man, who is the one who hears Jesus' words and puts them into practice. He is like a man who builds his house on the rock. His life has strong foundations which withstand storm and flood. The foolish man, however, builds his house on the sand: it's easy to build but shallow and so when challenged it comes crashing down. This is in harmony with Proverbs, as to live by his words is to find security in an unsteady world.

Changing the environment

Jesus also assured his disciples' anxious hearts by taking them for a walk on the wildside. He pointed them to the beauty of flowers and birds and their Father's care for them.

> Look at the birds of the air; they do not sow or reap or store away in barns, and yet your heavenly Father feeds them. Are you not much more valuable than they? Can any one of you by worrying add a single hour to your life?
> And why do you worry about clothes? See how the flowers of the field grow. They do not labour or spin. Yet I tell you that not even Solomon in all his splendour was dressed like one of these.
> Matthew 6:26-29.

The antidote to worry is to entrust themselves to their Father's care. It is to know that the King, who is over all, cares for them. Or, as we read in Proverbs, to live in the fear of the Lord. This way of life is secure, like a house with strong foundations, and also beautiful, like birds and flowers tended by their Father.

The beauty of the country or the seaside called out to many during Covid. During a time of restrictions, remote working actually allowed some the freedom to relocate. The ability for those who worked online to work from anywhere was an attractive prospect for those seeking to find that work-life balance. In Ireland this movement has been encouraged by the increasingly unsustainable cost of living in the capital city Dublin.

Everything isn't so rosy, however, in the garden of those who relocate. You can move to the beaches and enjoy the waves of the sea, only to be overcome with the work flooding your home and time. You can put yourself in the fresh air of the beautiful outdoors, but be distracted by the work that continues in your mind. Boundaries are needed for those who carry their work in their minds, and those boundaries take effort to construct.

The beautiful life that Proverbs and Jesus' teaching offers us involves hard work. A strong work ethic runs through the wisdom of Proverbs. The rewards of diligence and hard work are prized. The ruin of laziness and complacency are sounded as warnings. A lazy person's vineyard is over-run with thorns and weeds (Proverbs 24:30-34). The garden of life needs careful tending and weeding. Although it may seem like we find balance by easing back on overworking, you may be surprised to discover we need to work harder to see lasting change in our lives. Not in a sense of more hours at the office, but rather more work on our lives as a whole, as we are increasingly attentive and active in how we choose to live.

As we continue to move on, remote working seems to remain a viable option for many. Some workers will prefer a wholesale return to the office. Or could it be a blended way of working that mixes both? These decisions will require wisdom, both for employers and employees. Whilst the options appear clear, the decisions may be finely balanced.

The wisdom teaching in the Bible is a real help in the messy complexity of our lives. It is hard to simply summarise or categorise. It is firmly grounded and practical. As we seek wisdom to find our feet in the world, Jesus does not leave us short.

The Sermon on the Mount matches the wisdom of Proverbs in presenting a rounded understanding of who we are: more than heads and hearts full of knowledge and love, but also hands which work. We are more than just ourselves, but live in the round in God's world as we encounter friends and foes, family and neighbours, and most of all God himself. We are in conversation with the world, others, God, and ourselves: so there is wisdom for listening and speaking, for spending and saving, for working and resting.

It is within this world of wisdom that we find help in making decisions about our working environment. The strong work ethic of Proverbs offers us a surprising, but potentially more rewarding perspective on finding balance in our work. Rather than a movement towards working less, it tells us we need to work more. Not in a narrow sense of employment for which we are remunerated, but rather the work that sees real change in our lives. Change that is beyond our heads and hearts, but also seen in our habits.

Helpful habits

We need to direct the elephant. This is the picture used by New York University psychologist Jonathan Haidt.[14] He speaks of the elephant being the more emotional and subconscious part of our mind, whilst the rider on top is the more rational and conscious. These two aspects of our inner being can sometimes be in conflict, but he insists we now have ways of helping them work better together. Into this picture is added the paths, which are the habits we form, and along which the elephant will travel. So to see lasting change we need not only a change in our thoughts, but also of our desires and our habits. After all, if there's a struggle between the elephant and the rider, well it's pretty clear who is going to win!

An elephant on the charge is no laughing matter, but it did bring a smile to my face. I was hearing from a friend who was sharing his challenges in ministry for prayer. He was a pastor in Kenya and would cycle through the jungle to meet with Christian churches who gathered together to worship under a tree in their community. The danger was from the elephants. They hated the noise of the bikes. It frightened them and caused them to charge. The picture in my mind was funny, yet the risk to him was far from a joke. Indeed he shared how whole villages had been squashed flat by herds of elephants on the charge. I smiled as I considered how much we had in common in seeking to share Jesus with others, yet how different our contexts were.

Such is the power of our unruly hearts. Whilst, like the elephant, they need to be understood and directed to the path ahead, they can be helped by the paths cut by good habits.

In recovering my physical balance I learned to form healthy habits of walking and also doing exercises to improve my balance. There may have been a few near misses, like in hospital, but I managed to avoid any major moments or falls. Gradually over time my balance improved. Being in the company of family playing catch with me or breathing in the fresh air on walks no doubt helped, but partly the reward came with unglamorous and ordinary repetition. Through developing healthy habits.

In this period of my life, as I was unsteadied, I was able to regain balance beyond the physical. I was being challenged to be more roundly rebalanced through practising helpful habits. I seemed to feel the cold of the outdoors more deeply than before so I wrapped warm and kept on the move as I recovered in nature. I enjoyed recovering friendships and lengthening conversations, but had to learn how to notice when I had reached my listening and speaking capacity. I had hoped to lose some weight through a healthier diet and exercise and learned to balance the hungry evenings with the 'taste' of being healthy. As I recovered my heart and paid more attention to my feelings, I sometimes had to keep a journal to understand what was going on. I also learned new forms of prayer which helped me to hand my messy emotions over to God. I discovered the ancient practice of taking a phrase or verse from the Bible and repeating it in rhythm with my pattern of breathing out and in. I also learned to check in with my emotions and follow Bible verses, like pathways in prayer, to come to God. For example, I turned my worries into praise and prayer that I might receive peace, based on these verses:

> Do not be anxious about anything, but in every situation, by prayer and petition, with thanksgiving, present your requests to God. And the peace of God, which transcends all understanding, will guard your hearts and your minds in Christ Jesus.
> Philippians 4:6-7.

These habits were the pathway to delight, but they all took discipline. They had to be practised. Real change in recovering life comes with hard work. If we want intentionally to make more space for conversation with people, or to decrease screen time, or to make time to journal or pray, we will need to develop helpful habits. In this, we can be glad, we need not walk alone.

Jesus brought change in the lives of his disciples not only by teaching them but also by setting an example for them to observe and pattern their lives after. To walk in his ways. Jesus' Sermon on the Mount was spoken to those he called disciples; his followers, or pupils, or, even better, apprentices. They found wisdom not only in knowing information but also in practising Jesus' words. To be his disciple was not only to listen to his teaching, but also to be with him and see him in action, and then to be entrusted with work to be done for him. It was a wisdom learned in real life.

Broad wisdom

Jesus and Proverbs both call us to view ourselves in relationship with others. They prevent us from narrowly seeking quality of life for ourselves - while others suffer. The change of location some made during Covid was clearly not an option open to everyone. This highlights a pre-existing imbalance in privilege and choices available to different kinds of workers. Those who work in manual jobs, in retail or in hospitality were most affected by unemployment during Covid times and availed of income supports most. They lacked the same degree of freedom to relocate and work from home. There is certainly some imbalance here.

Perhaps even in reading this book you get the impression that recovering in nature, or with friends, or in our bodies, or especially in choosing what type of job will put food on the table is something available only to those who are privileged? If this is the case, can I ask you whether these aspects of a vision of life that is thriving should be available to everyone? If you think they should and they remain imbalanced, what can you do about it?

The wisdom of Proverbs continually draws our attention to those who are poor. Such sayings are a frequent feature of the book, such as,

Whoever oppresses the poor shows contempt for their Maker,
but whoever is kind to the needy honours God.
Proverbs 14:31

How can we be generous with what we have? Or perhaps a better question is how might we be just or fair? We could be fair by advocating for more just work and pay, perhaps for a living wage rather than the minimum. We could pursue fairness by voting for political representatives who would consider the least and address poverty. We could be equitable in sharing our plenty by giving to those in need.

Deep wisdom

Such wisdom is not only broad, but also deep. Jesus knew that changing habits would involve changing hearts. In the Sermon on the Mount, Jesus likens the heart to a treasure chest, "For where your treasure is, there your heart is also." (Matthew 6:21). He is calling his disciples to value what belongs to His kingdom over their material goods or money. He knows that what we love is what we follow.

So, as he introduces us to his heavenly Father who cares for birds and flowers, he invites us to trust him. As we read the accounts of Jesus in the Gospels, we discover that he is gracious and patient with the disciples. They certainly haven't written the gospel accounts to flatter themselves! Time and again they fail and fall, but Jesus restores them and gets them back on track. So they follow the one they love.

As I reflect on the counsel from the physio that my recovery would involve stretching myself, including the odd fall from over-reaching myself, I can say this proved true. At different moments in my journey I over-extended myself and had to step back and rest to recover. Such is the balance we need to find in life. It is far from a precise science. More an art that takes graft behind the scenes.

My life had been rearranged. I had been dislocated from my normal work rhythms. I was imbalanced and yet I was held. I discovered the delight of my Father's embrace. His love was steadfast even when I was off balance. Life wasn't a high wire act. It was a walk along a path. I had been rebalanced in the company of the, 'friend of sinners'.

The question at the beginning of Covid's storm was, "How might we still be standing in the end?" The path that lay ahead of me was surprising and yet it brought me somewhere new. In the end I was more than standing: I was also walking securely with him.

Poem - Strong

The mountains aren't for moving!
Rugged rockiness, resolute reliability.
Water falls, clouds carousel
Seasons change, they remain-

Established.

The seas aren't for stopping!
Roaring waves, noise and rage, Yet-
Trouble, tumult, turmoil turns
To picture perfect peace
Stilled.

Mountains move, quake and tremble
At your voice and our mustard seed faith.
Seas are stilled with a word
As faith is stirred, 'Who is this?'

Questions

1. In what ways have challenging times in life unbalanced you?
2. In the West we are top heavy, relying on our heads and not on our hearts or hands. What do you think of this idea? Where might you see signs of it working out?
3. The safest place to be is with the God who is not safe. How do you relate to the idea of the fear of the Lord offering security and beauty in life?
4. What might be some of the habits you would like to work on?

Prayer

O God our refuge,
might you shelter and strengthen us
in an unsteadying and unsafe world
Lord Jesus, accompany us on the path of life,
as we build our lives on your words,
renew our hearts and establish healthy habits
Holy Spirit, cause us to blossom like flowers
and fly free as birds under the care of our heavenly
Father.

CHAPTER 6

RECOVERING IN SEASONS OF LIFE

Wintering in Summer

**There is a time for everything,
And a season for every activity under the heavens
Ecclesiastes 3:1**

Sun drenched summer days warm our spirits. As children, the month of June saw excitement build, as we were on the brink of the summer. The teachers knew this too, as 'proper work' in school took a backseat. Sports days and school trips were the order of the day. We awaited freedom and fun with friends, dry days opening up the outdoors, long evenings and later bedtimes, the chance to get away and see somewhere new on holidays, to break up the routine and relax. This savouring of summer hasn't left me as the years have passed.

Freedom, fun and friends were especially welcome in the summer of 2020 after a time of restrictions. Getting outside our own four walls and our routines to somewhere different was greeted with enthusiasm. The selfie taken in the car, packed and raring to go, was full of broad smiles. Holidays, here we come!

One week in, the free flowing and joyful dance of

summer holidays was cruelly interrupted. Winter had come unannounced with the bleed on my brain. The seasons had suddenly changed. The harsh, cold, cruelty of life had made its unwelcome presence known. I was dancing no longer. Now I was sat down and wondering, "What's going on here?"

The winter of the first lockdown in Ireland arrived in the spring of 2020. It was an unseasonably sustained period of dry days and warm sunshine. This softened the restrictions as the garden of nature could be enjoyed. On the other hand, winter had arrived. The streets in town were quiet and stripped bare, like trees in December. The cool and harsh wind of this virus left us inside huddling for warmth and any comfort we could find. We were cruelly interrupted.

For many of us the hustle and bustle of our lives were brought to an abrupt halt. We were no longer chasing after progress and productivity, but were sat down to pause and ponder, "What's life all about?"

Meaning in the Meaningless

Life is full of unexpected and unwelcome interruptions. Disease and disaster are never too far away. The writer of the ancient wisdom book in the Scriptures, Ecclesiastes, reminds us:

> The race is not to the swift
>   or the battle to the strong,
> nor does food come to the wise
>   or wealth to the brilliant
>   or favour to the learned;
> but time and chance happen to them all.
>   Moreover, no one knows when their hour will come:
> As fish are caught in a cruel net,
>   or birds are taken in a snare,
> so people are trapped by evil times
>   that fall unexpectedly upon them.
> Ecclesiastes 9:11-12.

We are all subject to time and chance. We are all in the dark as to when disaster may strike. We are entrapped by evil times that fall out unexpectedly on us like a net.

We try hard to make sense of this. In Ecclesiastes, we join the teacher on a pursuit for some meaning and purpose in life. A quest that proves elusive and energy sapping.

"Meaningless! Meaningless!"
    says the Teacher.
"Utterly meaningless!
    Everything is meaningless."
Ecclesiastes 1:2.

"Meaningless" translates the Hebrew word, *hevel*, which can also mean elusive, transient, mysterious. It's like the mist rising off the ground on a winter's morning. Or like chasing the wind on a stormy winter's day. We can see it, but just can't seem to grasp it.

This word appears thirty eight times in the book of Ecclesiastes. We follow the teacher down countless avenues and dead ends. He discovers and discounts many sources of meaning, including wealth, job, status, and pleasure. His pursuit is nothing less than whole-hearted, but he returns empty-handed. Or perhaps empty-hearted?

Even when we struggle to make sense of life, that doesn't stop us trying! The early days of Covid lockdowns in the UK and Ireland saw some signs of an increased spiritual interest. People were praying and connecting to church more, as the internet allowed people to explore spirituality in new ways.

Being a pastor, I was encouraged by these early signs and wondered if people were seeking to put down roots, having been living on the shallow surface before?

Winter's barrenness

As we have become increasingly secular we are deprived of meaning in life. We are more prone to feel the chill of the wintering of life that Ecclesiastes describes. Could it be that when a crisis hits we seek deeper meaning because we are looking for warmth in the winter? For some kind of beauty beyond this barrenness?

The barrenness of trusting in economic assumptions of perpetual progress and productivity have been revealed by Covid calling. These models affect much more than the money in our pockets. They also inform our minds. Our lives are less straightforward and linear than we thought. Presumptions of slow and steady increase have been put aside. Rather there are seasons that come and go. Winter and then spring.

Winter's present beauty

The world is more round and round than our linear expectations. An observation that the writer of Ecclesiates seems at first glance to find wearisome.

What do people gain from all their labours
    at which they toil under the sun?
Generations come and generations go,
    but the earth remains forever.
The sun rises and the sun sets,
    and hurries back to where it rises.
The wind blows to the south
    and turns to the north;
round and round it goes,
    ever returning on its course.
All streams flow into the sea,
    yet the sea is never full.
To the place the streams come from,
    there they return again.
All things are wearisome,
    more than one can say.

The eye never has enough of seeing,
  nor the ear, its fill of hearing.
Ecclesiastes 1:3-8.

There is nothing new under the sun. Everything is on repeat. We are unfulfilled and unproductive. So, with coronavirus, winter had arrived bringing summer's flourishing into the ground. There is no gain from all our toil.

In this seasonality there is, however, also a welcome invitation to live in rhythm with the creation, to recognise:

There is a time for everything
and a season for every activity under the heavens:
a time to be born and a time to die,
a time to plant and a time to uproot,
a time to kill and a time to heal,
a time to tear down and a time to build,
a time to weep and a time to laugh,
a time to mourn and a time to dance.
Ecclesiastes 3:1-4.

We might even add - a time to summer and a time to winter. While naturally we welcome the second halves of these couplets with open arms, the writer invites us to receive the seemingly negative as also being beautiful.

He has made everything beautiful in its time. Also, he has put eternity into man's heart, yet so that he cannot find out what God has done from the beginning to the end.
Ecclesiastes 3:11.

God makes everything beautiful in his time. Yet this remains beyond our understanding. There is a strange beauty in this. We are called to trust that God is working beyond our understanding. Life issues forth from the work of his hands, not merely from the toil of our own.

There is more to life than progress and productivity.

In my journey of rest and recovery I welcomed this wintering. In many ways I had never felt lighter; letting go of work responsibilities as a tree sheds its leaves in winter, a leafless letting go. This felt freeing. Just as the ground lies fallow and the nutrients are digested underground from autumn leaves I was being fed in a deeper way. The hope of spring's restoration in my life filled me with hope, but it felt premature, there was beauty in this present winter gift.

I had learned to appreciate the present. Each day was unpredictable and uncertain. I greeted them with curiosity and a focus on the present day being enough. Receiving simple everyday pleasures were precious gifts. These everyday graces are described in Ecclesiastes in a world that is full of disaster and disease, that is hard to figure out, there is wisdom in receiving the gift of the present-

> I know that there is nothing better for people than to be happy and to do good while they live. That each of them may feast and drink, and find satisfaction in all their toil - this is the gift of God.
> Ecclesiastes 3:12-13.

Here are the warm rays of sunshine that might bring us some help and hope in the midst of winter.

Winter's painful beauty

From the earliest days of recovery in hospital I was trusting that God was in this. Even if I couldn't see fully what he might be doing. As my recovery unfolded I was able to quiet my spirit to this and to experience a contentment that was from beyond myself. A real help in this was a book called 'The Crook in the Lot' by Thomas Boston.[15] Its title comes from the wintry book of Ecclesiastes.

Consider what God has done:

Who can straighten
what he has made crooked?
When times are good, be happy;
but when times are bad, consider this:
God has made the one
as well as the other.
Therefore, no one can discover
anything about their future.
Ecclesiastes 7:13-14.

We find it more comfortable to consider how God straightens what is crooked, but these verses also invite us to trust him when he does the opposite. When he brings winter and not summer. So Boston's words helped me find God's beauty in winter - when my lot might be crooked, I could know that God was in it.

I decided to trust that God's hand had been at work in this period of being set aside. Even in this winter I knew the warmth of his good hand.

This didn't mean I had to pretend all I was experiencing was itself good. There was a crookedness to it. A cruel coldness at times, wintry. Yet I trusted it would be beautiful in his timing. Whilst I could discern the season, I couldn't fully grasp its meaning. I trusted God with what I couldn't fathom. I lived under his watch and care even when it was misty.

Yet he has placed eternity in the human heart. There is something in us that longs for the fog to lift. There is a desire for more than winter. Maybe this longing is even stronger at these times. The cooler we feel the more we seek the heat. Could it be the more secular our culture becomes, the hungrier and thirstier it is for meaning? Could it be when we find beauty in this world, it beckons us to something beyond? There must be more than this.

Such eternity is beyond this world and life under the sun, but what if he brought it to us? What if there was a warm, soft winter sun brightening a clear and crisp morning which came after the mist had lifted?

Light dawns on winter's dark

This is just how Jesus' coming is described in Luke's Gospel. He is the rising sun who has come to us from heaven, because of God's tender mercy (Luke 1.78).

In John's Gospel this new dawn is the bringing of light and life which is introduced as a new creation. In the beginning there is one who is God and is with God. Everything was made through him. So he is the source of light and life, just like the sun that gives light and warmth for plants and grass to grow to enable life on our planet.

> In him was life and that life was the light of all mankind. The light shines in the darkness and the darkness has not overcome it.
> John 1:4-5.

This light and life then comes into this world in the form of a person. He became flesh and dwelt among us. Just like the sunrise dawning, the light had come. Now we could see what God the Father was like, revealed by the Son, full of grace and truth.

The life that this new creation brings is described frequently as, 'eternal life' in John's Gospel. He has brought the eternity our hearts long for. This eternal life is defined like this, "...that we might know the only true God and Jesus Christ, whom you have sent." (John 17:3).

This eternal life is not only what awaits us beyond this world, beyond this time. Nor is it beyond our present bodies, which having wintered in death are sprung up to life. It is not a disembodied soul living with a disembodied god. Rather this eternal life and new creation has come in the person and the work of Jesus to meet us now. A foretaste of heaven has come to earth.

The Bible scholar, N.T. Wright, tells us that those in Jesus' time anticipated a new age coming.[16] They expected this to come after this current age. The remarkable thing about Jesus' coming is that the "life of the coming new age comes forward into the present in the person of Jesus." The eternal new age has dawned. Here is the gift of the present!

Filled with life

There is generosity in John's Gospel as he fills it with abundant pictures of the life that Jesus brings. Such generosity reflects that of God, who has shaped and filled his creation in a way that speaks of him.

The pictures of life that Jesus offers are found in the midst of our ordinary, everyday world. He is bread for the hungry, water to the thirsty, light in the darkness, a door to the searching, a way for the lost and the true vine for those who are barren. So in a wintry world, we have these rays of light which might illuminate something of Jesus to us. Or it might be better to say that these emblems can remind us of the spring that has dawned as the new life comes and thaws our world in Jesus.

So we can receive the present graces of food and work and family and friends who warm our lives in a wintry world. Yet we can go further and in this world detect some of the glory of God, especially as he has revealed himself in Jesus. In this we welcome the spring which comes beyond the winter.

So it was in my journey of recovery and rest that I found some of my deepest refreshing and renewal in getting hands on with these everyday things. To get out of my head and my thinking, and to get hands on in baking and cooking. To get hands on my guitar which had grown dusty and been neglected, but now strummed with life. Yes, I have no shame in admitting I was the cliche who, like so many others in lockdowns, took to sourdough and baking or took up an instrument. Yet this was more than a cliche for me. In engaging in these recreations I found a kind of spring dawning in me. Could it be that in being creative I was enjoying the closeness of the Creator, the great master craftsman of it all? Or merely finding my true self as someone made in his image? It seems winter was giving way to spring.

Life from death

The eternal life which John describes came through Jesus' death. Just as a seed dies in the ground to give life. This picture was used by Jesus in his teaching, "The hour has come for the Son of Man to be glorified. Very truly I tell you, unless a grain of wheat falls to the ground and dies, it remains a single seed. But if it dies, it produces many seeds." (John 12:23-24).

Jesus uses the ordinary, everyday seed to explain the life he will bring. Just as the seed dies to bring abundant life, so must he. Yet in doing this, the very rhythms of nature which winters before spring, bringing the death of a seed in the ground before it produces life, are shown to whisper something of Jesus before his coming. They anticipate him.

So Jesus wintered for us on the cross to bring us to summer. Such wintering is to be appreciated as beautiful and glorious in John's Gospel. The timing is fitting, the hour has come. Until this stage, 'the hour has not come' - it has been a constant refrain - the right time and season matter. The surprise is that it is the hour of death - of wintering - that Jesus is glorified. This wintering is beautiful. His love for us shines bright, as his life is sown generously in death. He makes everything beautiful in its time.

Jesus spoke these words to his disciples not only to explain his coming death, but to set the pattern which they were to follow.

> Anyone who loves their life will lose it, while anyone who hates their life in this world will keep it for eternal life.
> John 12:25

To find such life involves a death to living for ourselves - for seeking meaning only to fulfil ourselves. Rather when we come to Jesus he bids us come to die. To give ourselves for him and for others. In doing this we find life for ourselves. There is beauty in this wintering.

Such life is precious. Finding it is costly. As you've been making your way through this book there may be chapters and themes that stir you. You want to move towards this life in Jesus or to recover it more in practice. This will take sacrifice. Not everyone reading this book has the same choices open to them when it comes to their shape of living. We have differing amounts of money or opportunity or time on our hands. We may even feel trapped or helpless. Whilst this is all true, the greatest enemy and opponent to any of us recovering life is ourselves.

As I recovered my health, what alarmed me most was the number of people I shared my story with who knew their lives were too hurried. They loved the idea of recovering life. Travelling more freely, lightly, and slowly. They were feeling the winter and would long for the spring. Yet they refused to give themselves permission to pursue this. It seemed unachievable. Some even admitted to wanting to become unwell so they could have time to rest. They were unwilling to leave go of something more important. Whether it be reputation or significance or busyness or financial security or responsibility too great to be shared. They were unwilling to die… that they might live.

After winter, spring

In my recovery I felt a freshness that was heart and soul deep, as well as physical. A time of wintering had brought a springing of life.

As I write this chapter we have finally emerged from Covid's long winter, for the most part. The early appreciation for some of the beauty of leaving things go seems to have left us. Have you let things go in Covid times that have left you lighter? Or have we just picked everything up and picked up the pace again? For those who are involved in churches - how might you answer these questions. What have you let go? What have you picked up again? How have you wintered? Are there signs of spring?

After the winter of these secular times, roots may be sunk down deeper. As well as hostility to the Christian message today, there is also hunger for something deeper. Could it be that the shallowness of the secular story has left us longing for something deeper? After the winter, there could yet be spring.

Poem - Wintering

Winter came unannounced in a summer ambulance
Interrupting life's free flowing dance.
Frozen still, time is chilled in the ponderous present.
What seems ill turns to fulfil - the good that makes this Godsent.
Bereft and barren, stark and stripped,
veins and limbs exposed.
Bring light relief, just like the trees.
leafless letting go.
Fog and mist linger around 'From whence this came?'
'Where from here?'
Sharp blue skies, sharpen eyes to life in crystal clear.
Biting cold, rained inside, enclosed in windy storm
Flaming family and friends' love burns - their open fire warms.
Days are shortening, dusk and dark greet us all too soon,
Christmas light will shine bright, dispersing fear and gloom.
Spring is coming newlife hope, bringing joy and cheer,
Yet in this present winter gift, beautiful is here.
"He makes everything beautiful in it's time"

Questions

1. What season do you think you may be in right now?
2. In what ways have you known the barrenness and

beauty of winter in your life?

3. In these secular times how does Jesus offer hope and meaning?

4. What might be some actions you need to take to die so that you might live?

Prayer

Lord of light and life
who, like a seed, died that we might have life
might you take our wintering in this world
and warm us with your present graces,
and brighten our barrenness with the beauty of your eternal life
That in our wintering we might know spring.

CHAPTER SEVEN

RECOVERING IN THE DARK

Living (and laughing) in the Dark

**When I looked for light,
Then came darkness
Job 30:26**

Laughing in the dark

If you didn't laugh you'd cry. It was only meant to be an overnight stay in hospital. The next day was to bring a straightforward test that would be the gateway to getting on with my life. I was now six months post-bleed on my brain and had recovered well. I was glad to begin work with the church again. The circle of health and energy and life was expanding. Until now all tests had shown no abnormalities as the source of the bleed on my brain. This test offered the prospect of confirmation of this fact. A chance to put this chapter behind me. It turned out somewhat differently.

I'd been delayed getting a bed on the ward and then my test was rescheduled, being displaced for others of higher priority. So I continued to wait over the weekend. When the time came, the radiologist carefully navigated a catheter around my blood vessels, releasing dye and collecting images. "Breathe normally," he said. I was holding my breath, in anticipation of what this might bring. His initial impression was he may have seen something, but would consider the images more carefully.

My team of neurosurgeons informed me of the news that an abnormality had been discovered. I had a tangle of blood vessels called an AVM (arteriovenous malformation). It was likely that this was here from birth and was only discovered now. It had been hiding away beneath the blood from the haemorrhage in previous scans. The good news was there were some options available to address this and prevent a recurrence of the bleed. The most scary, yet most effective, way of dealing with this was surgery. So the doorway to freedom had changed to preparing for the doorway to the operating theatre.

All of this was in the midst of Ireland's third wave of Covid when we were topping the world's charts for all the wrong reasons. The meaningful Christmas we had been promised, and some had obviously enjoyed, and the UK variant had got together to ruin our party. Cases were on our ward and on the minds of the staff, many of whom had suffered, and were returning to work themselves.

It was no laughing matter, yet comedy prevailed. The good humour of staff and patients together in the ward gave courage and brightened the bleakest of Januaries. I'll save the blushes of the main actors by sparing the details, but in our six bed bay were a band of unlikely brothers and one sister that you would struggle to find together in any other setting. Together in our difficulties we became the most unlikely comedy club. We supported each other through the twists and turns of our journey by keeping our spirits up. There was laughter at professional levels of snoring, stealing one another's food, and staff nurses' names being comically mispronounced. All this was done with the dark and dry Dublin humour that beautifully levels everyone and yet lifts them at the same time.

As I underwent a number of scans to map out my brain for the surgery, scheduled for a few days' time, I was keen to get back to the ward where I knew my dinner was under threat of being eaten! As I got to the ward, thankfully, the dinner was still there and a much needed package of clothes had arrived in the post. Just as I was enjoying the curry and rice, I was visited by my consultant who changed the plan. I was to be discharged home. Surgery was postponed for now. The rising cases of Covid in the hospital made it too risky. So, the package of fresh clothes reached me just in time for me to pack them up and take them home. Darkly comedic timing!

For those familiar with the stress and stark suffering encountered in the shadow of death in hospital settings this will be no surprise. Humour is a vital weapon, in the war to brighten the darkness and bring much needed hope, and indeed healing.

The dark - no laughing matter

We aren't used to death calling at the door. In our modern Western world we have managed to avoid suffering and death remarkably well through the wonders of medicine. We keep death closed away in hospitals. Confined, by and large, to the distant land of old age, as life expectancies have increased. The reality is that it is more present than we recognise or care to admit even in the most normal of times. In the midst of Covid we were being given numbers of deaths on a daily basis. In truth this was only the number of Covid deaths, never mind the others. In more normal times we live oblivious to such harsh realities. The pandemic had brought death to our doorstep.

Sadly it also disrupted our customs around death which bring comfort. It distanced us from the dying and grieving in the cruellest fashion. Family members could not be physically present with their loved ones to say goodbye. So healthcare staff took on a heavier burden of care in giving vital emotional and relational support. As funerals were restricted to small numbers of family, the comfort and consolation of the community were sorely lacking. Times were dark indeed. Where was the hope?

There are of course those who look to brighten death's darkness by finding hope in religion. Whilst it may bring some comfort, if even those who have faith suffer, we might question what help it really brings. 'Surviving Covid', a Channel 4 documentary, showed Pastor Tobi whose strong faith didn't shield him from several strokes and failed kidneys that led to him being discharged home with severe mental and physical disabilities.[17]   He had survived Covid, but had to live with harsh consequences. He was dealt a blow so heavy he can hardly speak or lift his head.   It seemed like even God had left him in the dark.

Tobi's story resembles that of Job in the Bible. This book, that is thought to be one of the oldest in the Bible, deals with the age-old question of suffering. As we are introduced to Job he is one about whom God boasts-

> There is no one on earth like him; he is blameless and upright,
> a man who fears and who shuns evil.
> Job 1:8.

This doesn't spare Job from suffering.   Instead he suffers in the most horrendous way.   This extreme test reveals Job's continued commitment to count God worthy of worship even when his face doesn't shine on him.

As he loses his family, his wealth, and then his own health he refuses to curse God, but continues to worship him.   This is the lofty vision we have from chapters one and two of Job.   We listen in on the conversation in heaven.   A perspective on suffering from above.   From these heights we quickly descend into the valley of suffering for the majority of the rest of the book (from chapters three to thirty-seven).

This takes us to particularly dense poetry in which Job voices his pain and suffering, and some (so-called) friends add their voice and only worsen his pain.   As we read the daunting, mysterious and puzzling jungle of Job, it matches the daunting, mysterious, and puzzling jungle of life, faith, and suffering. His pain is immune to easy and neat answers, even though his friends are ready with them.

At first glance his friends may speak a lot of sense. There are many truths in what they say. Their neat and tidy theology and presumption that Job's suffering is a result of his sin, are called out by God in the end as false.

Job, on the other hand, suffers not only physically, but also relationally. He is isolated and feels betrayed not only by human friends and family, but most painfully of all - by God himself. Yet he still cries and wrestles and struggles with God. His words often sail close to the wind. He borders on the blasphemous. In the end he regrets and repents. Remarkably, God commends him as speaking right, not his friends.

Job is far from silent in his suffering. In this there is a welcome invitation to cry out to God in our anguish and suffering. To question and to vent and lament. To pursue him even in the darkest valley.

Denying the dark

Unfortunately in my own recovery journey I was slow to accept this invitation. I was much happier quieting my spirit in the fear of the Lord outlined in Ecclesiastes. To trust myself to what he was doing beyond my knowing.

There was something that nagged me though, and drew me into the wisdom of Job. If I'm being honest I hadn't darkened Job's door too often in the past. I was afraid of being entangled in suffering. Scared of venturing into the deep dark. Sadly this denying of the dark only allowed deeper agitations to foster.

I never felt the need to wrestle with God or doubt what he was doing, but as I lived with the messy emotions associated with hidden brain injury I was frustrated and sore. Rather than wrestle with God I ended up struggling with myself internally, or with my beloved at my side. My spirit was agitated. I'd been rubbed up the wrong way by suffering. Sadly this led me to take my soreness in suffering out on Ally who was just as sore caring for me through this.

I was struggling with communication and emotions and, at times, I felt isolated. No-one seemed to understand. I wanted to be known and loved, yet in my suffering I felt others were in the dark about what was going on. The words of Job helped me voice this darkness and release this wrestling.

I wonder if in our culture today we might be just as prone to deny the dark? We distract or divert ourselves with entertainment or find relief in the creature comforts at hand in our consumer culture. We avoid suffering and death at all costs. In the end, disease and the decline to death catch up on us. To deny this is only to find ourselves on a slippery slope.

In our secular story, this world is all there is. It may at first glance appear that life is a flat line. We come into the world and make our way through until we reach the full stop. We're on the level. Yet we actually follow the arc of tragedy, in which the story ends in a downer. We are born and grow into our lives and find ourselves up the hill of significance and success. At some stage we will descend and then decline to death. When we're in the middle of our lives in this story, suffering is to be avoided at all costs, as it only sends us down the slippery slope. So we avoid it. We deny the darkness.

Beyond the dark, light

To deny the dark, in this way, is to miss the hope that finds light in the valley full of shadows. After all, it's always darkest before the dawn.

Amidst the darkness of his suffering, something in Job looks for the light beyond. There is a spark of hope in the thickest darkness.

At least there is hope for a tree:

> If it is cut down, it will sprout again,
>   and its new shoots will not fail.
> Its roots may grow old in the ground
>   and its stump die in the soil,
> yet at the scent of water it will bud
>   and put forth shoots like a plant.
> But a man dies and is laid low;
>   he breathes his last and is no more.
> Job 14:7-10.

Job is experiencing death in his body and yet as he observes the tree, something doesn't sit right within him. How can trees be renewed and humans can't? That can't make sense can it?

So he reaches for something more. He puts out roots towards life and says:

> If someone dies, will they live again?
> All the days of my hard service,
>   I will wait for my renewal to come.
> You will call and I will answer you;
>   you will long for the creature your hands have made.
> Job 14:14-15.

He anticipates a day coming when life will be renewed and, as he continues to say in v.17, his sin will be sealed up in a bag and covered.

In the dark, this small yet significant spark, is further fuelled into the blazing fire of faith that can say:

> I know that my redeemer lives,
>   and that in the end he will stand on the earth
> And after my skin has been destroyed,
>   yet in my flesh I will see God;
> I myself will see him
>   with my own eyes—I, and not another.
>   How my heart yearns within me!
> Job 19:25-27.

In saying this, Job could be leaning forward into his own physical renewal in this life after his skin has been diseased. Yet it does appear to stretch further, as his voice in the darkest of places gives some of the brightest hope of life beyond death that we have in the Old Testament. Perhaps he speaks beyond what he knows? These words are more than his own, as they are part of the Scriptures, God's inspired word. So God speaks hope into our darkness.

In the end Job's fortunes turn around. There has been a turn-up for the books. Not only is his life recovered and restored, but it overshoots where he has been before.

The LORD blessed the latter part of Job's life
more than the former part.
Job 42:12.

This book, which is one of the darkest and starkest descriptions of suffering in the Bible, is a comedy. No, you're not mistaken, I did just say that this darkest of writings is a comedy. Obviously the content is no laughing matter, but the shape of the story is U shaped, so it follows the trajectory of a comedy, in classical terms. It is upturned. This story of Job, hope in the darkest suffering, resembles the story of another righteous sufferer, the crucified Jesus.

Mark's account of Jesus' life focuses on his death and has been described as a story of Jesus' passion with an extended introduction. He emphasises Jesus' death. His style is stark and straight, and so he presents Jesus' death as his darkest day, as he details the suffering of the cross. In the middle of this day nature hid its light, as if in shame at this the ultimate travesty of justice as the innocent one suffered. Yet this is no ordinary suffering or death. In this daylight darkness there is hope.

Whilst certainly being no laughing matter, Mark builds up layers of irony as he communicates the crucifixion.

The mocking soldiers who crown someone as King, but who looks anything but. The title above the cross claiming he is the King of the Jews. The irony being that in his suffering the King, promised by God to come to the rescue, has the unlikeliest of coronations. He was a King who came not to be served but to serve and to give his life as a ransom for many. So it was through the darkness of death that he brought the light of life.

This light dawns as some women of faith go to the tomb early in the morning to discover Jesus has risen from the dead. Such news will spread in a way that brings a hope filled faith to many, but is initially greeted in the strangest, yet most honest of ways. The women are trembling and bewildered. They flee from the scene and say nothing to anyone because they are afraid. This dramatic turning point had turned their lives upside down.

Such resurrection hope would, in time, make sense and settle into the early Christian worldview, aided by an encounter with the risen Jesus, before his ascension. It shaped their worldview as comedy not tragedy. It was smile shaped, not frown shaped.[18] This upturned smile anticipates an ending that makes all the difference to living the messy middle of life.

A different type of living

Such hope met me in the dark following my surgery being postponed. Although it was better that my AVM had been brought into light so it could be addressed, I couldn't help feeling I was in the shadows. As we considered surgery, I was drawn initially to the risks more than the reward. I felt my mortality in a new way, as I recognised I had been living with this weakness all the time since my bleed, unknowingly.

As I considered afresh options to address the AVM, I found my hope in the valley of the shadow of death. In this darkness I knew the promise of the familiar Psalm 23, that he would be with me through the valley, so I need not fear.

On the whole my story has been more fitting with Psalms of trust or those that celebrate God's deliverance. As my health has recovered, this chapter has been a comedy in its trajectory, if not its content. Indeed, as a family, we have faced a number of significant health challenges which have all been in the shape of a smile. We have faith stories to tell of God's deliverance.

As I consider the sweep of the Scriptures and the stories of God's people who have suffered, this is not always the case in this life. There is, in this life, loss and lament. There are also those whose fortunes don't seem to turn upward. They face a prolonged valley of suffering in this life. They have chronic health struggles.

This is the story of Sharon Hastings, a doctor who has not only medical understanding of severe mental illness, but personal experience of it. Her initial diagnosis was made as a medical student. Remarkably she sat her finals as an inpatient. Her rollercoaster journey from then has sadly meant she has never practised as a doctor. As she released her book, 'Wrestling with my thoughts' in 2020, she describes a different kind of hope. "It is not a book about healing but it is a book about hope" Sharon says. "I have not recovered. My illness is there and I deal with it every day. I'm very aware that God can heal but he does not always… I'm coming to terms with the fact that it is God who gives me strength."[19]

Sharon is one among many whose full recovery is unrealised. Whilst there may be ups and downs, there is a prolonged walking in the valley. The hope Jesus brings gives strength to put one foot ahead of the other.

The Christian story reaches for a hope of restoration beyond this life. Just as Job sent out roots reaching for renewal beyond the here and now. The stories of those whose recovery awaits beyond this life, yet whose hope gives strength in difficult days, show a different way of living.

This is different from the story of secular materialism. Let me suggest that this view of life, where we find fulfilment only in the here and now actually leads to lives of quiet disillusionment, detachment, and darkness. This ending to our story serves to leach the light and life from our everyday.

A different type of dying

The bleed on my brain saw me closer to death's door than I'd ever been before. Yet strangely in the initial days of recovery I felt safe and secure. Having to face the reality of death has a way of stripping away everything that is unimportant. It brings things into the plain light of day. There were so many shadowy unknowns. What had caused this? Would I recover fully? Would it happen again? Would I need surgery? Yet there was a security found in the reassurance of a recovery of life beyond death, because of Jesus. The upturned ending of the Christian story gave me an upbeat attitude even in this darkest moment. I was able to laugh and be positive because of what lay beyond.

Today we are actively preparing to deal with our anxiety and fear, to cultivate resilience and positive mental health. What if the danger and death which causes our fear could be removed? Just as effective vaccines proved a real game changer with Covid, imagine if death itself was defeated so we might fear it no more. This is the astonishing claim of the Christian gospel. That death doesn't have the final word. We don't descend into death in the end, but trusting in Jesus, we can rise to life. This makes all the difference to living and to dying.

So, we don't need to deny the dark. If God can work through the darkest of days and the death of his Son to bring the light of life, what does that mean for our darkest days? It is just like him to be at work in our darkest moments and difficulties. Even at death's door to bring his hope.

We might even dare to laugh in the dark. We can even dare to smile at death's door. For recovering life, in its fullest sense, lies on the other side.

Poem - God in the Dark (Job 38-41)

God stronger
God stranger
God before and beyond
Our worst and wildest danger
Silenced! Silent.

Silent the Lion of Judah's roar,
To silence death's rage forevermore-
He lives!
Stronger and stranger, before and beyond our worst
and wildest danger.
He lives!

Questions

1. When have you been able to brighten the dark with humour?
2. How often do you find yourself thinking about death?
3. How might the death of Christ bring us hope?
4. Christian hope makes a difference to our living and dying. Who can you think of who has displayed this hope?

Prayer

Strong God, whose ways our not our ways,
Whose thoughts are not our thoughts,
We give thanks that you are greater than
Our worst and wildest dangers,
Lord Jesus, the Lion of Judah, who suffered and was silenced
for a while in death that you might silence death's rage,
We give thanks that you are alive
We trust that, in you, death does not have the last word.

CONCLUSION

Are we there yet?

**But the Lord God called to the man,
"Where are you?"
Genesis 3:9**

Our kids have grown up with the excitement of road trips. Visiting family involves a three or four hour journey in the car. The joy of being with the people you love seems to energise the journey. There are a few helps along the way, the backseat is full of various toys and games and books and screens and snacks for the journey. Added to this is the excitement of stopping at the services for something to eat. They genuinely greet all of this with the spirit of adventure. Indeed, when asked what he most looked forward to at Christmas 2020, my eldest son drew a picture of the car journey to family.

The view from the front seat is somewhat different. I normally take the easy option by driving! Ally literally has her neck turned with requests from the back. These are accompanied by the moments of frustration and irritation that inevitably find their way out. (Normal enough, I reassure myself). So it seems the journey isn't all about enjoyment, but a fair bit of endurance as well.

Into this heady mix of excitement, the dreaded question emerges, "Are we there yet?" There is nothing as annoying as the continued repetition of this question. A constant reminder that we've still a road to travel. To be fair, as the kids have grown older, they now recognise the landmarks and understand the timings more. They are better equipped for the journey.

As we come to the close of this book about recovering life the same question hangs in the air, "Are we there yet?" The journey this far has brought us through the freshness of the garden, in the company of good friends and conscious of our bodies. We have found life for our faint hearts, balance in our work, an appreciation of our timings, and hope for our darkest days. We've covered some ground. I hope some of the sights and scenes have given you a vision for a way of life that is hopeful and life giving. There may be an optimistic enthusiasm for the road ahead. It would be normal enough though, to be greeted with the unwelcome reality that there's still a way to go in recovering life.

In another way you may feel like the journey hasn't even got going. This book may have been a chance to pull off the road and to reflect. To walk around the different aspects of our humanity, as natural, relational, physical, emotional, vocational beings who travel through different seasons and sufferings in our lives. This could be compared to a self assessment on a wheel of wellbeing. A health check-up. Where to from here?

Recovering my health

As I write this conclusion I am glad to have recovered well. There are now over three years between me and the bleed on my brain. I have left behind me the physical symptoms of dizziness, imbalance and fatigue. The hidden brain injuries, including challenges with concentration, emotions, communication, and difficulties with noisy environments, have also fallen away, almost completely. Almost. There are still times when I am more tired or strained, that they come to call in lesser ways. I'm certainly not where I was. For this I am glad.

Nor am I completely back to normal. I prefer to say

I've recovered well. In honesty I feel like I'm in a different place now than I was before. In many ways I am healthier and fitter than I was before. In other ways I have found a different way of going. I am more conscious of my own body and its varying degrees of energy, which I manage and put to use more flexibly than I used to do in the past. I am happy my capacity has increased to levels that allow me to work hard for prolonged periods. It also allows me to engage in periods which are busier and more stressful. Yet I have learned to find balance and I rest, retreat and recover more promptly. For these lessons on the recovery road I am grateful.

Yet it takes an effort to hold on to them. As I awaited surgery to remove my AVM, truth be told, I didn't look forward to the recovery. I know that's rich coming from the author of a book entitled, 'Recovering Life'! I enjoy my energy and didn't relish the thought of being sat down again to rest and recover. Being honest there are also the risks that surgery brings. For a period, these anxieties got to me.

Until my beloved, at my side, reminded me of the road I'd travelled before. She helped me appreciate afresh how God had been with me. The road for recovery for me, in the fullest sense, led through a hospital and an operating theatre before a better life out the other side. A journey she reminded me, I do not make alone.

I am glad to say I have since received this surgery and recovered well. I await some follow up tests, with the hope I can soon put this all being me. I look forward to getting on with leading a happy and healthy life in the sweet company of those I love. Yet there is something in me that is afraid I will let go of the lessons I've learned. Whilst you are recovering your health there is an obvious safety device to the hectic life. Your energy can only go so far. Those around you recognise you are recovering. You have a ready excuse and permission to take better care of yourself. As I will feel increasingly back to normal in coming days, then will be the true test to see if I'm really there yet. How much will I have learned when I am out in the open expanses of life again?

Recovering our life

As we increasingly put Covid behind us, I wonder if we're back to normal? Have we bounced back? This may well be an unrealistic expectation. Debbie Hawker, a psychologist who has written on resilience, explains how resilience has been described as the ability to 'bounce back'.[20] She doesn't like this definition as it doesn't do service to the nature of recovery, for those who have suffered burnout. They don't bounce back. Neither are they back where they were before, but rather have come to somewhere new. This matches my own recovery of health. So I wonder, as we collectively recover life following all that Covid has brought our way, isn't it unhealthy to act like nothing ever happened? To pretend we've bounced back?

Obviously you've a fair degree of tolerance when it comes to the topic of that particular virus. You likely have a healthy appetite for reflection too if you've picked up this particular book. Yet it's easy to be swept along without reflecting on what this time has offered to us and taken from us. Are we any different? Hustled. Hurried. Hectic. From whence we came, are we destined to return?

Just as we get into the clear air beyond this virus, the world is rocked by news from Ukraine. Russia is on the move. War in Europe the scale of which has not been seen since World War Two. The world is far from steady and safe. Again we are being shaken. In this way Covid was unremarkable. It was just one among a series of shakings that we face in life, although its scope and spread were unusual. We were all facing the same stormy sea, at the same time, even if not in the same boat.

Has anything changed? It doesn't seem we are any less anxious and fearful as a society. Steadiness and strength seem to be a way off yet.

We're certainly a distance from the vision of the great

garden at the end of the Bible. Trees with leaves for healing. No more viruses. No more war. No more fear. We definitely aren't there yet. However this new creation or eternal life has come to meet us here and now. Whilst the broken world around us waits for its restoration, we can carry a healing and wholeness in ourselves.

Recovering our faith

We carry it in ourselves, but it doesn't come from ourselves. The path to recovering life is not found in self-help, self-improvement or even self-discipline. It doesn't lie in returning to the hurt, caused by judgmental, moralistic religion. Nor does it lie in being swept away by the secular tide, rootless and restless and all at sea. Rather there is a surprising invitation issued by the one who himself is called, 'the Life'.

This invitation is issued by a doctor to those who know they are sick to come with him on the road to recovery. This is just how Jesus describes himself as he is found at the table surrounded by so-called sinners. The self-help religionists are incredulous. How could a holy man be so tainted? Jesus' answer is life-giving:

> It is not the healthy who need a doctor, but those who are ill.
> I have not come to call the righteous, but sinners to repentance.
> Luke 4:31-32.

Jesus was unafraid to offend those who considered themselves spiritually well. He reached out to help those who knew they were spiritually sick. Like a doctor he invited people to recovery by repenting.

To repent is to decisively turn away from our own path and to follow God's. It is to change the direction we are travelling. It is seen in practical obedience. It begins with turning towards Jesus and trusting him to forgive our sin and so heal us spiritually. It also continues in a process of being transformed into Jesus' likeness and following his footsteps.

In turning to Jesus and trusting in him, there is an instant change that occurs in our identity. We, who were once spiritually dead to God, are now spiritually alive. (See Ephesians 2.1-10). We desire to know him and to live in his ways, when previously we were following our own desires and appetites and incapable of changing ourselves. Through Jesus' death he has brought us to life. We have been regenerated. Made new. Even when it mightn't look like it or we mightn't feel like it. This is our standing before God because of Jesus.

The journey of recovery that Christians walk in this life is to become more of who we truly are. It is to live out the reality of this radical new identity. This gradual growth in becoming like Jesus and walking in his ways is called sanctification. It is to be holy or, 'Jesus-kind-of-different'. This is, in one sense, a journey of recovery that we will be on until we die or until Jesus comes again.

Your own recovery

If you are someone who has begun this journey with Jesus let me finish with a refreshing reminder that he is the doctor, who invites you on a road to recovery. You may wish you were further ahead than you are. You may feel condemned or filled with shame or guilt as you have read this book. If you feel your sin, be encouraged, Jesus came for people just like you. Your sin doesn't take him by surprise.

Forgive me for being seemingly cheeky, but without knowing you, I can confidently say, you're not there yet. Neither am I. None of us are. We are all on the road to recovering the life of Jesus in us. Let's keep going. Who could you be in conversation with as you walk this road? How can this move from your thoughts and feelings, and into your doings?

Maybe you're someone who hasn't committed yourself to Jesus. Let me invite you to take a closer look at who he is. Reading one of the Gospels for yourself would be a great place to start. The Gospel of John is full of life and would seem especially in sync with this book. This could feel like something you need to check out yourself. Or you could be in conversation with others, especially those who follow Jesus themselves. There are good resources for reading John's Gospel together with a Christian friend.[21] Another option would be to join an Alpha or Christianity Explored course where your questions will be welcomed in the midst of a community investigating Jesus together.[22] You might not be there yet, but let me encourage you to take the next step.

We're here!

So we've reached the end of the road. Well, the end of this book anyway. Thanks for joining me on the journey. Wherever your path leads from here let me offer you the blessing below, as a prayer, as you take your next steps.

Let me close by inviting you to be grateful for where you are at this moment. There's a road ahead, but you've come this far. Take a deep breath, relax, and receive this present gift. You're here!

An Irish Blessing for the road. (Author unknown).

May the road rise to meet you;
may the wind be always at your back.
May the sun shine warm upon your face
and the rain fall softly on your fields.
Until we meet again
may God hold you
in the hollow of his hand.

ACKNOWLEDGMENTS

This book has been some time in the making. The inspiration behind it belongs mainly to the first six months of recovering from my bleed on the brain. The writing and shaping have been over a longer period of three years of a health journey, which in numerous ways has taken longer than I might have hoped. It was no time for deadlines. I wrote as windows of times unfolded in front of me, in waiting for this, and then for that, and then for the other. It was during this time, as creativity flowed, that all of the six poems I penned, which are included in the book, were written.

In another sense, this book has also been written out of an even longer recovery of life, which is my spiritual formation as a disciple of Jesus. This goes back to at least my childhood (recognising that my own family roots and story have huge influence too). In writing, and recovering, and growing as a Christian, I have been a slow learner, but can now appreciate time as a friend, rather than the enemy. The road has been long, but I have not walked alone.

As I set out to acknowledge some of the people who contributed to this book more specifically, I recognise how wonderfully unable I am to express credit and thanks to the marvellous multitude of people who have helped me on the road to recovering my health and to growing in faith in Jesus. To such a crowd who have joined me, and helped me on my way I am thankful.

This book began as a series of entries on my blog, as I enjoyed the free flowing creativity of writing as my strength increased.[23]   The spark of the book idea was fanned into flame by a number of conversation partners who inspired me on my way. A few that come to mind are a comment from Lindsay, a long chat in the park with Tony, a walk by the sea with Paul and Isabel.

As I got working on my first draft I sought the help of two trusted friends, themselves gifted with words and lovers of books, who I could trust to give me early and honest feedback.   David Wilson and Andrew Dawson, thanks for putting in the hard work of reading the early drafts, digging in with me, as I laid down foundations on which to build.

At various stages along the way I was the recipient of generosity from authors, who offered me some time and wisdom.   Whether it was making time to chat or giving some helpful tips and advice, thanks to Peter, Rick, Seth, Alan and (another) Tony. An extra helping of thanks also to Seth Lewis whose two poems feature at the end of chapter two.

There were also a handful of people who were brave enough to give up some of their summer to read a draft and offer feedback.   Thanks to Avril, David, Jean, Janice, Kathryn, Sarah, Tony (the first one mentioned) and Uel. Thanks also to some of the feedback gleaned in offering the book to a number of publishers for consideration along the way.   It turns out what was hardest to hear was probably also what refined my writing the most.

I'm very grateful to have found Paul Coulter and PESIOD Publications and to work together on this book. I love the vision for PESIOD and hope it might become a help to many more authors in making more good books available.[24] Paul, for your careful and considered editing, I am very thankful.   Sometimes the free-writing poet in me was launching out with words in a way that was unclear, or making connections that strayed beyond what might be trusted or true.   Thanks for helping the writing flow, but also keeping it faithful.

I have Paul Davies to thank for the cover design. Thanks for making the time during your studies and family life to craft this. Whilst I know we should never judge a book by its cover, I suspect I have refused the invitation offered by many a book by doing just that. You've managed to create a cover that is inviting and captures well the sense of what the words inside convey. As you formed the stump and the shoot for the cover, little did you know that Job 14:7-10, which paints the same image of hope, is included in chapter 7 of the book. A fitting image not only of my own recovery, but also more broadly of the irrepressible hope of the gospel, which will rise afresh even if our culture seeks to cut itself off from its Christian roots.

I'm grateful for the keen eye for detail of Christine Memory, who generously gave of her time in proof-reading at more than one point in the process! Thanks for helping me be consistent and clear.

Also to all those who have recommended this book, or reviewed it, or helped to promote it in any way, thanks for your efforts.

Although I accept responsibility for any wild and wacky ideas that may have been found in this book, I refuse to claim sole ownership of anything that is trusted and true. As a disciple of Jesus I have been a learner who has grown in community. To my church family in Ferrybank Christian Community Church, and my mission family in European Christian Mission, thanks to all who I've been listening to and learning from and alongside in these years.[25] Thanks also for the trust shown in me that time spent in writing was not a threat to my responsibilities in leadership, but rather an extension of connecting and communicating the gospel of Jesus. Some of the wisdom that has made its way unto these pages has formed part of my teaching across the past few years. Thanks for the encouragements and the conversation that continues as we grow as disciples.

Coming near the end now, as I turn to my family, whom I love, beside me and behind me. The words of this book come from my Mum, who is a lover of language in poetry and reading, as well as ready encouragements of those by her side. They also come from my Dad, who is a keen observer of life and who is unafraid to ask questions which go against the flow.

At the beginning I dedicated this book to my wife, Ally, who has been steadily at my side in the shadows. She has been my constant companion in my recovery over the past few years. As well as taking more of her fair share of the weight in parenting, she has also continued to let her light shine in creatively and compassionately contributing to our church family. I really do pray now might be your time to shine, although I recognise you never really stopped shining even in this season of shadows.

To my children, Anna, Eoin and Conor, nothing brings me as much joy as seeing you grow and thrive in life. The sharing of many a meal and story around our table are much of what feeds and nourishes me on my way in life. It took me some time in life to find my confidence and creativity, and to allow it to flow freely. My prayer for you is that you might find your confidence and creativity in life, in Jesus. Might he be the companion on the best of your adventures and your comfort in your sorest of sufferings.

Finally I offer these words, this season of recovery, and indeed all my life to Jesus.

For to me, to live is Christ and to die is gain.
Philippians 1:3.

ENDNOTES

Introduction - How did it come to this?
1. Ian McShane (2019) 'Ireland of 2019 is very different from the one we surveyed 10 years ago', *The Irish Times*

Chapter 1 - Recovering in Nature.
2. RTE Press Centre (2022) 'Vitamin Sea', Available: https://presspack.rte.ie/2019/04/01/vitamin-sea/
3. Jefferson Bethke, To Hell with The Hustle (Nelson Books, 2019)

Chapter 2 - Recovering with Friends.
4. Sean Moncrieff, *The Irish Paradox* (Gill and Macmillan, 2015)
5. Sherry Turkle (2012), 'The Flight from Conversation', *The New York Times*
6. https://sethlewis.ie

Chapter 3 - Recovering my Body.
7. Nancy R. Pearcey, *Love thy Body* (Baker Books, 2018)

Chapter 4 - Recovering our Hearts.
8. Scott Berinato, 'That discomfort you're feeling is grief' interview with David Kessler, 23 Mar 20 - https://hbr.org/2020/03/that-discomfort-youre-feeling-is-grief
9. Adam Grant, 'There's a name for that blah you're feeling - languishing', Dec 2021, New York Times - https://www.nytimes.com/2021/04/19/well/mind/covid-mental-health-languishing.html
10. Steve Hoppe, *Sipping Saltwater* (The Good Book Company, 2017)
11. John Calvin, *Commentary to the Psalms*, https://www.ccel.org/ccel/calvin/calcom08.vi.html
12 *Unbroken,* directed by Angelina Jolie (Universal Pictures), 2014

Chapter 5 - Recovering our Balance.
13. *Man on Wire,* directed by James Marsh, (2008) Icon Film Distribution in UK.
14. Jonathan Haidt, The Happiness Hypothesis (Basic books, 2006)

Chapter 6 - Recovering in Seasons of Life.
15. Thomas Boston, *The Crook in the Lot* (Christian Focus Publications, 2012).
16. NT Wright video, 'Is the gospel of John really about eternal life?' https://www.youtube.com/watch?v=WDFfewWoTS4

Chapter 7 - Recovering in the Dark.
17. 1 *Surviving Covid,* documentary on Channel 4, first shown 2 Dec 2020 - https://www.channel4.com/programmes/surviving-covid
18. Glen Scrivener, Divine Comedy - Human Tragedy: What is Life? (10Publishing, 2018)
19. Sharon Hastings, 'Wrestling with My Thoughts' in Vox Magazine - https://www.vox.ie/001/wrestling-with-my-thoughts

Conclusion- Are we there yet?
20. Debbie Hawker on Leadership Journey Podcast with Alan Wilson. https://podcasts.apple.com/gb/podcast/the-leadership-journey-podcast-debbie-hawker-on/id1318645931?i=1000548956336
21. www.theword121.com
or if you're in Ireland check out, 'What's The Story, John' on www.whatsthestory22.ie
22. www.alphaireland.org or www.christianityexplored.org

Acknowledgments
23. https://waitingforbrandnewday.blogspot.com/
24. https://www.pesiod.com
25. https://ferrybankchristianchurch.ie
https://www.ecmi.org/en/

Printed in Poland
by Amazon Fulfillment
Poland Sp. z o.o., Wrocław